Handbook of Old Pottery

and Porcelain Marks

Pie Plates. Red Earthenware with Sgraffito decorations. American, about 1800, made by
David Spinner, Bucks County, Pennsylvania. *Courtesy, Brooklyn Museum.*

Dish. Porcelain. Marked with monogram "C.A.C. and Belleek". American 1889-1896,
made by Ceramics Art Co., Trenton, N. J. The Ceramics Art Co. was the immediate pre-
decessor of Lenox. *Courtesy, Brooklyn Museum.*

HANDBOOK OF OLD POTTERY & PORCELAIN MARKS

BY C. JORDAN THORN

FOREWORD
BY JOHN MEREDITH GRAHAM II

TUDOR PUBLISHING COMPANY
NEW YORK

MANUFACTURED IN THE UNITED STATES OF AMERICA

CONTENTS

ILLUSTRATIONS

Frontispiece. Pie Plates. Red Earthenware with Sgrafitto decorations. American about 1800, made by David Spinner, Bucks County, Pa.

Dish. Porcelain. Marked with monogram "C.A.C. and Belleck". American 1889-1896, made by Ceramics Art Co., Trenton, N. J.

1. Jug. Pottery. English (Liverpool), late 18th Century.

2. Toddy Jug. Chinese Lowestoft, late 18th Century. Decorated with arms of the United States.

3. Porcelain group. Danish. Youth and Sleeping Shepherdess. Copenhagen, about 1783.

4. Dish. Worcester Porcelain, with scene from Aesop's Fables. English, 18th Century.

5. Teapot. Porcelain. English Worcester, about 1770-1775.

6. Plate. Chelsea "Lacework", dating from the 1770's.

7. Plate. English, Staffordshire, 19th Century, with Clews' *Dr. Syntax and the Bees.*

8. Figure. Merchant. German Porcelain. Frankenthal, about 1760.

9. Ornament of Birds. Porcelain. English Chelsea, late 18th Century.

10. Pair of Candlesticks, Chelsea. showing a shepherd teaching a pretty shepherdess how to play a pipe. Dating 1765-1770 and illustrating the "bocage" or background of leaves.

11. Chinese export porcelain, with the arms of the State of New York. Late 18th Century.

12. Plates. Chelsea and Chelsea-Derby, showing a few of the many types of decorations used.

13. Figure of man. Type known as "Ramlagh Figure". English Crown Derby, 1765.

14. Figure of Benjamin Franklin. English, Staffordshire, by Enoch Wood, (1759-1840).

15. Teapot. Decorated in Chinese style. English, Worcester, about 1770.

16. Soup Tureen. Salt Glaze. English, 18th Century.

17. Breakfast set, Sevres porcelain. Second half of 18th Century.

18. Teapot. Salt Glaze, with portrait of the King of Prussia. Staffordshire, about 1705.

19. Vases. Royal Sevres porcelain, 1782 and 1789. Paintings within the medallions by Dodin.

20. Group. Chinese on horseback. German porcelain, modeled by F. A. Bustelli, Nymphenburg, about 1757-1762.

21. Pitcher. Porcelain. American, made by William Ellis Tucker, Philadelphia, Pa., 1828-1838.

22. The Duke of Cumberland, represented as a Roman Emperor. By Ralph Wood, about 1770-1780.

23. Sweet-meat dish. White earthenware, 1771-1772, by Brown and Morris, Philadelphia, Pa. Capital "P" in underglazed Blue.

24. Meissen. Early mid-eighteenth Century, with characteristic decoration.

25. Jug. Stoneware. American, 1818-1830, made by Daniel Goodale, Hartford, Connecticut.

26. Vase cups, with medallions of Cupids. English Chelsea porcelain, circa 1765.

27. Teapot. White salt-glazed stoneware. Designed by Daniel Greatbach and made by American Pottery Co., Jersey City, N. J. 1840-1850.

28. Lion. Flint enamel earthenware with cole-slaw decoration. Designed by Daniel Greatbach, made by Lyman Fenton & Co., Bennington, Vt.

29. Pottery Figure, Eloquence, English (Burslem) about 1787, by Enoch Wood.

30. Statuette groups. Soft paste porcelain. English Chelsea, showing William Pitt receiving the gratitude of America. 1765-1775.

31. Pitcher. Rockingham glazed earthenware, rope design on handle, about 1845. Made at Salamander Works, Woodbridge, N. J.

32. Pitcher. Porcelain, about 1830. Made by Smith, Fife & Co., Philadelphia, Pa.

33. Majolica dishes. Italian, Sixteenth Century. Gubbio ware; Urbino ware; Deruta ware.

34. Three pieces of Bennington ware. American, 19th Century.

35. Figurine of a Lohan-Buddhist praying man. Three-color Tz'u Chou ware, Chinese, late Sung Dynasty, 960-1280 A. D.

36. Hard paste porcelain. Figures of mountain miners. German, Meissen, Kandler 1740-1750.

37. Biscuit. Sevres, French, by Louis-Seniore Boizot (1743-1809).

38. Biscuit. Another group. Same maker as above.

39. Tin-enameled Majolica, lustred Italian, Deruta, about 1530.

40. Majolica plate. Italian, by Francesco Xanto Avelli de Rovigo. Urbino, lustred at Gubbio. Dated 1531.

41. Sugar Bowl. Tin-enameled, soft paste porcelain. Chantilly, 1725-1735.

42. Sauce boot and mug. Soft paste porcelain. English, Lowestaft, 1780 and 1800.

43. Pot-pourri vase. Soft paste porcelain. French, Sevres, 1757.

44. Vase. Soft paste porcelain. English, Chelsea, about 1760.

FOREWORD

Few phases of art have had more universal appeal throughout the world than ceramics. From the early period, when European production secrets were carefully guarded under royal patronage to the present time of specimens designed by individual artists, there has been a constant interest in the makers and their marks. This interest has reached a high point in the United States where there is to be found a greater diversity of ceramics from all parts of the globe than in any other one country. The vast assemblage of ceramics in America commenced in the colonial period with importations made by wealthy merchants, planters and public officials who were eager to possess specimens of European and Oriental wares. With the advent of tea and coffee the demand increased and sailing vessels arrived in American ports with large cargoes of ceramics. Popular among the number was Chinese Export porcelain and it was not unusual for an individual to order from China an entire dinner service decorated according to special design.

The American market eventually became such a factor that European makers produced wares bearing American scenic views, state coats of arms, important personages and events. Conventional patterns were also made in quantity that met with popular favor in sectional parts of the country.

Early attempts were made to produce ceramics in the United States beginning with the settlement of Jamestown, Virginia in the 17th century and continuing with varying success until today. Many of the American products show a strong European influence just as the designs of European wares were in turn often copied from earlier Greek, Roman and Oriental specimens. American ceramics, like American furniture, silver, and glass, have a distinct and individual quality of their own, and cannot be considered imitations of European examples.

Recently many facts have been brought to light through research of old records and by excavations of early pottery sites which have made it necessary to re-evaluate the field of American pottery and porcelain for a thorough understanding of the subject.

For some time there has been a real need for a book of ceramic marks within the means of all who are interested in this phase of art. The Handbook of Old Pottery and Porcelain Marks by C. Jordan Thorn is a worthwhile contribution toward this end.

The American section of the book contains the most comprehensive list of marks that has appeared to date, with some new material that should be of interest to ceramic collectors.

JOHN MEREDITH GRAHAM II

INTRODUCTION

In this effort to bring together in one concise volume thousands of pottery and porcelain marks of more than 25 nations, the author has limited the information on the various manufactories to that which is pertinent to the monograms or marks presented. Much could be said historically of many of these factories, but that is not the purpose of this work. It is, rather, an attempt to condense into a readily accessible and simplified form, a complete listing of all known marks, initials and signatures of pottery and porcelain works throughout the world. It is designed as a useful guide for collectors, dealers and students, one which will enable the interested to ascertain the origin of their pottery and porcelain by means of the markings found on the base of the pieces.

Easy reference has been provided to each mark in conjunction with the basic information on each factory. As much as possible, each mark has been treated as a separate entity and in most cases specific dates and names are given. The method of marking has also been included and can be differentiated, roughly, as follows:

IMPRESSED: Stamped in the body of the ware while it is still soft.

INCISED: Drawn by hand in the body of the ware while it is still soft.

UNDER-GLAZE IN COLOR: Painted by hand under the glaze. Limited to blue.

OVER-GLAZE IN COLOR: This includes those marks stamped, printed or painted on the exterior of the glaze.

Only a limited amount of information has been presented under the notices on Japan and China, for the following reasons: (1) The subjects are vast and complicated. (2) The presentation for the reader would necessarily be tedious and confusing. (3) Nothing could be compiled on the marks of either nation that could improve upon what has already been published by numerous authorities.

The various grades of pottery and porcelain have been categorized and defined as simply as possible, in order to avoid confusion on the part of unknowing readers. The several types are divided in the following manner:

PORCELAIN: A translucent ceramic ware generally white and usually glazed, characterized by a clear ring when struck. Soft paste and hard paste compose the two types of porcelain. Soft paste porcelain can be scratched by any sharp instrument, leaving a soft powder, while hard paste resists the workings of a tool of this sort. A granular fracture is presented by soft paste, while hard will leave a smooth, curved surface at the break.

POTTERY: This term includes all wares distinguished from porcelain by being opaque and generally formed of colored clay. (Earthenware, Fayence, Stoneware, etc.)

EARTHENWARE: Broad term including all pieces made of clay and then baked. (Delft, Fayence, Stoneware, etc.)

BISCUIT or **"BISQUE"**: White, unglazed porcelain usually found in the composition of groups and figures.

DELFT: A colored, tin glazed earthenware frequently blue and white, made first in Delft, Holland.

FAYENCE or **FAIENCE**: A variety of glazed pottery usually highly decorated in colors. The term is now applied loosely to cover all kinds of artistic pottery, including majolica and delft.

MAJOLICA: Highly decorative, glazed pottery.

STONEWARE: Hard, impermeable, glazed earthenware.

It will be observed that under the heading of "Germany" data will be found on some factories actually lying outside of Germany proper. The unsettled condition of Europe today precludes a permanent national classification for many manufactories. The author has, therefore, seen fit to include under "Germany" those works that were Germanic in character, and, more specifically, those of the Germany-Austria-Hungary group.

The period of years covered by this work extends roughly from 1400 to 1900. Information on the more important factories dating after 1900 will also be found. A large majority of marks shown belongs to the 18th and 19th centuries, which is as it should be, for the great interest in collecting today lies in the wares of this period. Specimens produced before this time are comparatively scarce and, accordingly, knowledge of many of these early manufactories is rather obscure. Generally, however, the reader will find that all of the material compiled is as complete and definite as possible, with a notable exclusion of irrelevant facts.

For many years there have been collectors of eighteenth century porcelain, and, in consequence, therefore, new factories have come into existence in the twentieth century to produce imitation products of the authentic early factories. The marks on these imitation products are, as often as not, correct. To deal with the difference between the genuine and the fake is outside the realm of this book, but the discerning collector will readily recognise a fake when he sees one. However, the author has endeavoured to state, wherever possible, the type of porcelain used by the various factories, i.e. Chelsea used a soft paste, whereas the imitation products of this factory are made in a hard paste. If the student is in doubt as to authenticity of a piece of Chelsea, he has but to examine the porcelain itself. This book is primarily a guide to marks. Other knowledge must come from experience and study.

In the preparation of this work many authorities had to be consulted and much of the material was verified by leading experts in the various fields. The author is particulary indebted to Mr. Frank Stoner, the leading authority on English porcelain, for checking that section of the book and to Mr. David Rosenfeld for applying his vast knowledge of German porcelain to reading and correcting the proofs. For the interest shown by Mr. John M. Graham II of the Brooklyn Museum, undoubtedly the greatest authority on American pottery, it would be impossible to completely repay in gratitude.

C. JORDAN THORN

BELGIUM

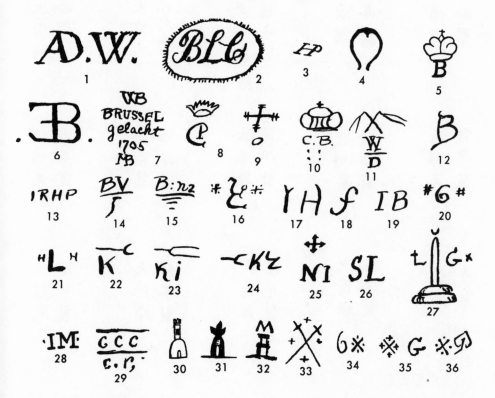

Ardennes, Namur (1-2)

Late 18th or early 19th century.
1 A. D. Vander Waert.
2 B. Lammens & Co.

Bruges (3-4)

Established late 18th century.
3
4

Brussels (5-26)

The initials of L. Cretté, a manager, are
found occasionally.
5 Schaerbeek, near Brussels (1784-
1791).
6 Etterbeek, near Brussels (1775-
1803).

7-26 Various marks on Flemish
fayence.

Liège (27)

A fayence manufactory was carried on
here from 1752 to 1767.
27

Malines (28)
28

Tervueren (29)

Established about 1720.
29

Tournay (30-36)

Established 1750. Absorbed by Boch
Bros. in 1850. Frequently the mark
BOCH FRERES impressed.
30-33 1750-1850.
34-36 Boch Bros.

CHINA

大明弘治年製 5　大明成化年製 4　大明宣德年製 3　永樂年製 2　洪武年製 1

大明天啟年製 10　大明萬曆年製 9　大明隆慶年製 8　大明嘉靖年製 7　大明正德年製 6

大清乾隆年製 15　大清順治年製 14　大清康熙年製 13　大清雍正年製 12　崇禎年製 11

大清同治年製 20　大清光緒年製 19　大清咸豐年製 18　大清道光年製 17　嘉慶年製 16

Ming Reign-Marks (1368-1643)

1 Hung Wu (1368-98)
2 Yung Lo (1403-24)
3 Hsüan Tê (1426-35)

7 Chia Ching (1522-66)
8 Lung Ch'ing (1567-72)

11 Ch'ung Chêng (1628-43)

Ch'ing Reign-Marks (1644-1909)
12 Shun Chih (1644-61)

16 Chia Ch'ing (1796-1820)
17 Tao Kuang (1821-50)

4 Ch'êng Hua (1465-87)
5 Hung Chih (1488-1505)
6 Chêng Tê (1506-21)

9 Wan Li (1573-1619)
10 T'ien Ch'i (1621-27)

13 K'ang Hsi (1662-1722)
14 Yung Chêng (1723-35)
15 Ch'ien Lung (1736-95)

18 Hsien Fêng (1851-61)
19 T'ung Chih (1862-74)
20 Kuang Hsü (1875-1909)

DENMARK

1

2

3

Copenhagen (1-9)
Porcelain factory founded 1760. Three wavy lines in blue under glaze. Fayence works existed here in early 18th century.
1 1775 to present day
2 Found on revivals of old productions.
3 From 1889.

6

4

5

4 Bing & Grondahl. Established 1853.
5 Uncertain mark.
6 1760-1768. Frederick V.

8

7

9

7 Naestved. H. A. Kahler.
8 From 1853. Bing & Grondahl.
9 1753-1770. On fayence. Jacob Fortling.

FRANCE

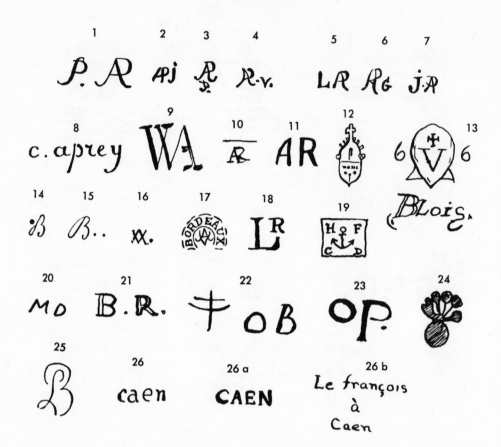

Aprey (1-8)
Established around 1750. Fayence.
1-8

Apt (9)
Factory of fayence here around 1750.
9

Arras (10, 11)
Soft paste porcelain. 1782-1786.
10, 11

Beauvais (12)
Existed in 14th century.
12

Blois (13)
Fayence factory in 17th & 18th centuries.
13

Boisette (14, 15)
1777 to about 1792.
14, 15

Bordeaux (16-18)
Founded about 1784.
16, 17
18 Latens & Rateau after 1828.

Boulogne (19)
Established around 1857.
19

Bourg la Reine (20-24)
Established 1773 to about 1814. Pottery after 1814.
20-22 On porcelain.
23-24 Later marks on pottery.

Brancas Lauraguais (25)
Existed 1764.
25 Occasionally date is inscribed.

Caen (26-26b)
1798 to about 1810.
26, 26a.
26b 1st half 19th century. M. Le François.

4

FRANCE

Chantilly (27-29)
Founded in 1725. Soft paste porcelain.
27, 28 Marks in blue or red.
29 Marks of M. Pigory after 1802.
Choisy le Roi (30-31)
30 Porcelain. Established 1786.
31 Fayence. H. Boulanger & Co.
Clignancourt (32-40)
Established 1771. Porcelain.
32 1771-1775. Windmill in blue.
33
34 Mark in blue.
35 1775-80. Mark in red.
36 L.S.X. Initials of the Prince in gold.
37 Mark in red.
38 "D" for Deruelle, founder.
39 This mark used to about 1790. In red.

40 About 1779.
Creil (41, 41a)
Established in 18th century.
41, 41a Marks impressed.
Crépy en Valois (42,43)
1762-1770.
42, 43 Marks incised.
Desvre (44)
Up to 1732.
44 Dupré Poulaine.
Etiolles (45, 46)
Established 1768.
45, 46 Monier et Pellevé.
Fontainebleu (47-50)
47 Jacob Petit. Established 1790.
48, 49 Fayence. 17th century.
50 Godebaki & Co. Since 1874.

5

FRANCE

Gien (51)
Established about 1864. Majolica.
51 Mark stencilled.
Goult (1, 2)
1740-1805.
1, 2 Marks on fayence.
La Rochelle (2a)
Established 1743.
2a J. Briqueville.
La Sienie (3, 4)
Established 1774.
3, 4
La Tour d'Aigues (5, 6)
Before 1773 to 1793.
5, 6
Le Montet (7)
Late factory of stoneware.
7
Lille (8-17)

Existed in 1696. Porcelain after 1711.
There were numerous factories here
producing fayence.
8-11 Francois Boussemart. 1729-1778.
Fayence.
12
13 1784 to about 1792.
14-16 14—On porcelain. 15—F. Boussemart. 16—Fayence.
17 19th century porcelain.
Limoges (18-52)
First porcelain factory here in 1773.
Haviland & Co. founded in 1840.
18-20 J. Pouyat. Earthenware.
21-23 1773-1788 Hard paste porcelain.
24-26 Marks of late Limoges factories.
27-31 Late Haviland marks.

6

FRANCE

Limoges (Cont'd)
32-52 Late marks of miscellaneous Limoges factories. 39—M. Redon.

Lunéville (1-3a)
Fayence factory established in 1731.
1-3 Keller & Guerin. From 1778.
3—Recent mark.
3a P. L. Cyffle. From about 1768. Biscuit.

Marens (4, 5)
Fayence factory from 1740 to 1756.
4, 5 J. P. Roussencq.

Marseilles (6-20)
6-11 Joseph Gaspard Robert from about 1766 to 1793. Porcelain and fayence.
12-13 Veuve Perrin. Fayence.
14 Antoine Bonnefoy. Fayence.
15 Fauchier. Fayence.
16-18 H. Savy. These marks after 1777.
19 Savy. Mid 18th century fayence.
20

Martres (21)
Fayence.
21

Marzy (22)
Fayence factory established 1850.
22 T. H. Ristori.

FRANCE

The marks shown above include the following numbered ceramic marks (23-67 and 1-12):

23, 24, 25, 26, 27, 28, 29, 30, 31

32, 33, 34, 35, 36, 37, 38, 39

40, 41, 42, 43, 44, 45, 46, 47, 48

49, 50, 51, 52, 53, 54, 55, 56

57, 58, 59, 60, 61, 62, 63, 64

65 (MOUSTIERS), 66, 67 (a moulins)

1 (J. Boulard a Nevers 1622)

2 (1636), 3, 4 (F.R. 1734), 5, 6, 7 (HB 1689), 12 (de conrade A neuers)

8 (H·B 1689), 9 (S.), 10 (P·C), 11 (E.Borne 1689)

Mathault (23)
Fayence factory established 18th century.
23

Meillonas (24)
Established about 1745.
24 On fayence.

Ménnecy, Villeroy (25)
1735-1806. Both fayence and porcelain. Mark is painted or impressed.
25 Initials of Duc de Villeroy, patron of the factory.

Moustiers (26-66)
1686-1800. Fayence.
26-48 Joseph Olery. 18th century.
49-66 Miscellaneous 18th century marks.

Moulins (67)
18th century fayence.
67

Nevers (1-12)
Fayence. Existed in 16th century. Many factories here in the 18th century.
1 J. Boulard.
2 Denis Lefebvre.
3 Jacques Bourdu.
4
5 Circa 1700.
6 Haly.
7, 8 Henri Borne.
9 Jacques Seigne. 18th century.
10
11 Henri Borne.
12 Domenique Conrade. 1650-1672.

FRANCE

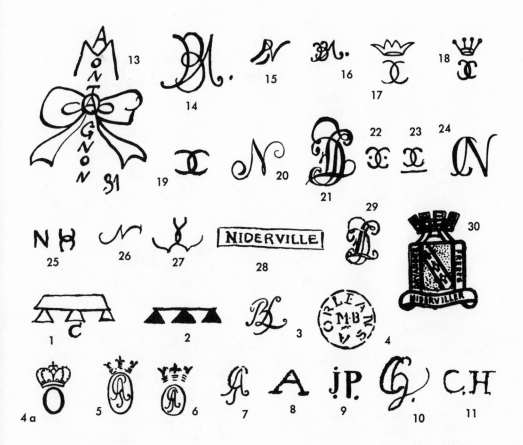

Nevers (Cont'd)
   13 M. Montaignon. Late 19th century.
Niderviller (14-30)
   Established 1754. Pottery and porcelain.
   14-16 Baron de Beyerlet period. 1754-1780.
   17-20 General Count Custine period. 1780-1801.
   21 Monogram (F.C.L.) of M. Lanfrey. 1802-1827.
   22-27 Custine period. 1780-1801.
   28, 29 M. Lanfrey. 1802-1827.
   30 M. L. G. Dryander. From 1827.
Orléans (1-4a)
   Fayence and porcelain factories established in 1753.
   1 Soft paste porcelain.
   2 Hard paste porcelain.

3 Benoist le Brun. 1808-11. Initials in gold or blue.
4 On earthenware figures.
4a
Paris: (5-28) (1-15)
   Angoulême (Rue de Bondy) (5-8)
      1781-1829. Hard paste porcelain. Marks in red or gold, either stencilled or painted. Founded by Dihl & Guerhard
      5-7 Angouleme Guerhard.
      8 1793 or later.
   Belleville (now Fontainebleu) (9)
      Established in 1790 by Jacob Petit.
      9 Mark in blue.
   Chanou, Henri (Faubourg St. Ant.)
      Established 1784.
      10, 11 Henri F. Chanou.

FRANCE

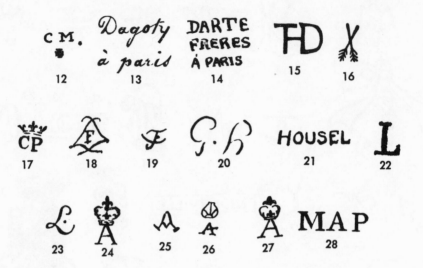

Paris: (Cont'd)

Chicanneau (12)
Until 1762.
12

Dagoty (13)
Established late 18th century to 1820.
13 P. L. Dagoty. Mark in red.

Darté (14)
Founded 1796.
14

Deck (15)
Established 1859. Fayence.
15 Theodore Deck.

Dubois (16)
Founded about 1773 by Vincent Dubois.
16 Mark in blue.

Faubourg St. Denis (17)
Started in 1769 by Pierre Hannong.
17 "C.P." for Charles Philippe, the patron of the factory.

Feuillet (18, 19)
Existed about 1820.
18, 19 Mark in gold or black.

Guy & Housel (Formerly Leboeuf) (20, 21)
Existed up to 1804.
20 Guy & Housel.
21 Housel (1799-1804).

Lassia (22, 23)
Established 1774 by Jean Joseph Lassia.
22, 23

Leboeuf (Porcelaine de la Reine) (24-27)
Established 1778 by André Marie Leboeuf. Successors were Guy & Housel.
24-27 Mark in red. "A" for Marie Antoinette.

Morelle (28)
Established 1773.
28 Morelle à Paris. Stencilled or stamped.

FRANCE

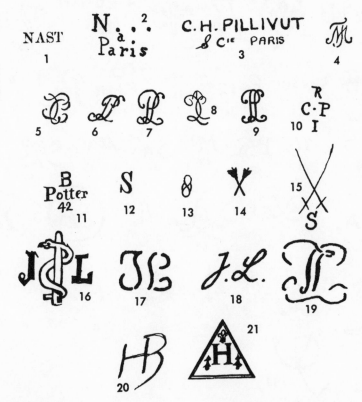

Nast (1, 2)
Started in 1783. Closed 1835.
1, 2 Marks in red.

C. H. Pillivuyt & Co. (3)
Established about 1817.
3

Pont-aux-Choux (4-9)
1784-1806.
4 1784-1786.
5-9 1786-1793.

Potter (Prince of Wales' China) (10, 11)
Established 1789.
10, 11 In blue and red.

Rue de la Roquette (Souroux) (12, 13)
Founded 1773.

12, 13 "S" for Souroux.

Rue Fontaine au Roi (De la Courtille) (14)
Established 1773.
14 Mark in blue.

Samson (15)
Made clever imitations of works and marks of all the important factories.
15 Old Samson mark.

Premières (16-19)
Established 1783.
16-19 Dr. J. Lavalle. 19th century.

Quimper (20, 21)
Factory established 1809.
20, 21 La Hubaudiere & Co.

FRANCE

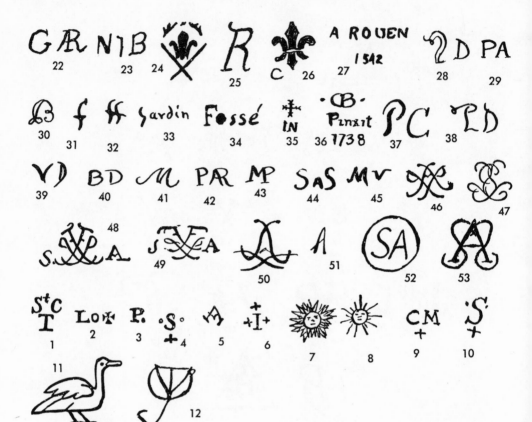

Rouen (22-45)

Existed in 16th century. Numerous factories have been established since then.

22 Guillebaud. Circa 1730.
23 N. J. Bellenger. 1800.
24-32 Miscellaneous.
33 Nicolas Gardin. About 1760.
34, 35
36 Claude Borne. 1738.
37 P. Caussy. Circa 1720.
38 Circa 1722.
39 V. Dubois. Circa 1800.
40 B. Duprey. Circa 1800.
41 Circa 1720.
42 c. 1720.
43 P. Mouchard. c. 1756.
44 c. 1760.
45 M. Vallet. c. 1756.

St. Amand les Eaux (46-53)

Started about 1740. Soft paste porcelain factory established in 1800.
46-51 Early marks on fayence.
52-53 Later marks on porcelain.

St. Cloud (1-10)

Before 1670 to 1773. Fayence and porcelain.
1 Henri Trou, after 1722.
2-6 4 and 6 uncertain.
7, 8 1696-1732.
9 After 1711.
10 Uncertain.

St. Porchaire (Henry II or Oiron) (11, 12)

1520-50. No. 12 is the only mark known.
11 A design in the decoration.
12 Scratched under glaze.

FRANCE

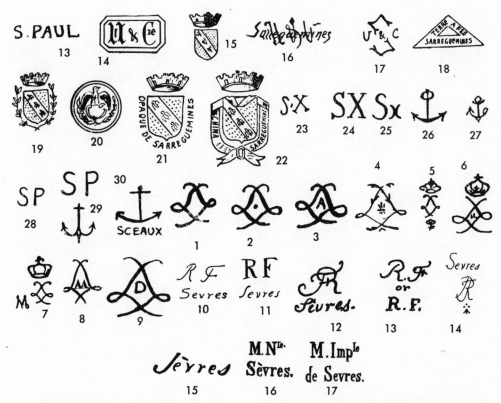

St. Paul (13)
Fayence. 18th and 19th centuries.
13

Sarreguemines (14-22)
Established about 1770 by Paul Utzchneider.
14-22 These are 19th century marks found on fayence and porcelain.

Sceaux Penthièvre (23-30)
Fayence factory established about 1749. Porcelain was made after 1775. Ceased as an art factory in 1795.
23-25 1772-1795. Richard Glot.
26-30 After 1775.

Sèvres
Factory formerly established at Vincennes in 1745 was removed to Sèvres in 1756. Soft paste porcelain was made until 1769 when both soft and hard were produced. The quality of the work fell off after 1793. From 1890 to 1904 date was generally omitted from mark. Sèvres also noted for its fine biscuit, which was not marked until after 1860. Marks until 1793 were generally in overglaze blue. Many imitations of these early marks are found.

1, 2 Early Sèvres or Vincennes. Before 1753. These marks were occasionally used after this date.

3 1753. This mark was faked on later wares made in the Sèvres factory and also on modern pieces made elsewhere.

4 Early Sèvres.

5-7 Crown over interlaced "L" used on some pieces of hard paste porcelain.

8 1778.

9 1756.

10-14 1793-1804.

15 1793-1800.

16 1801-1804.

17 1804-1809. In red.

13

FRANCE

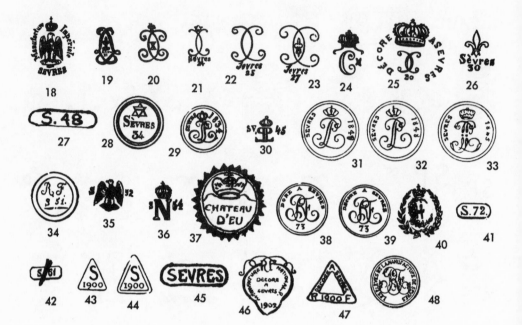

Sèvres (Cont'd)

18 1810-1814. In red.

19 1815-1824. Generally in blue.

20-23 1824-1829. Generally in blue.

24 1829-1830. Used on pieces only gilded.

25 1829-1830. Used on decorated pieces.

26 1830. In blue.

27 Used since 1818. 48 represents year 1848.

28 1831-1834. In gold or blue.

29 1834. Usually in blue. Louis Philippe.

30 1834-1848. Usually in green.

31-33 Louis Philippe. From 1834.

34 1848-1851.

35 1852-1872. Usually in red.

36 From 1852.

37 On royal services for various chateaux.

38 1872-1879. Mark shows year of gilding. In red.

39 1872-1879. Mark shows year of decoration. In red.

40 For Catherine II of Russia.

41 1872.

42 Issued in 1861 undecorated.

43 1900-1904 and later.

44 1900-1904 and later. Impressed on biscuit.

45 1860-1899. Impressed on biscuit.

46, 47 These marks indicate year of decoration.

48 1890-1904. In red.

FRANCE

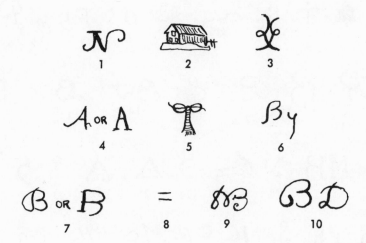

1 2 3

4 5 6

7 8 9 10

Sèvres (Cont'd)

The following is a list of the marks and monograms of various painters, decorators, and gilders at Sèvres.

First Period
1753-1800

1 Aloncle, F.—Birds, animals, emblems, etc.
2 Anthaume—Landscapes and animals.
3 Armand—Birds, flowers, landscapes.
4 Asselin—Portraits, miniatures, etc.
5 Aubert—Flowers.
6 Bailly—Flowers.
7 Barré—Detached bouquets.
8 Bardet—Flowers.
9 Barrat—Fruits and flowers.
10 Baudouin—Ornaments, friezes, etc.

FRANCE

Sèvres (Cont'd)
1 Becquet—Flowers.
2 Bertrand—Detached bouquets.
3 Bienfait—Gilding.
4 Binet—Detached bouquets.
5 Binet, Mde.—Flowers.
6 Boucher—Flowers, garlands, etc.
7 Bouchet—Landscapes, figures, ornaments.
8 Boucot—Birds and flowers.
9 Boucot, P.—Flowers, birds.
10 Bouillat—Flowers, landscapes.
11 Bouillat, R.—Detached bouquets.
12 Boulanger—Detached bouquets.
13 Boulanger, son—Pastoral subjects, children.
14 Bourdois—Sculptor.
15 Brachard—Modeler.
16 Bulidon—Bouquets.
17 Bunel, Mde.—Flowers and bouquets.
18 Buteux, senior—Flowers, emblems, cupids.
19 Buteux
20 Buteux, son—Detached bouquets.

21 Buteux, son—Children and pastoral subjects.
22 Capelle—Friezes.
23 Cardin—Detached bouquets.
24 Carrier—Flowers.
25 Castel—Birds, hunts, landscapes.
26 Caton—Pastorals, portraits, children.
27 Catrice—Flowers and bouquets.
28 Chabry—Miniatures, pastoral subjects.
29 Chanou—Bouquets, flowers.
30 Chanou, J. B.
31 Chapuis—Flowers, birds, etc.
32 Chapuis, son—Detached bouquets.
33 Chauveaux—Gilding.
34 Chauveaux, son — Detached bouquets, gilding.
35 Chevalier—Flowers, etc.
36 Choisy, De—Flowers and arabesques.
37 Chulot—Flowers and arabesques.
38 Commelin — Detached bouquets, garlands.

FRANCE

FRANCE

Sèvres (Cont'd)

1 Barbin—Ornaments.
2 Barré—Flowers.
3 Barriat—Ornaments and figures.
4 Belet, A.—Ornaments.
5 Belet, E.—Flowers.
6 Belet, L.—Ornaments.
7 Beranger—Figures.
8 Bienville—Ornaments.
9 Blanchard, L.—Gilding.
10 Blanchard, A.—Ornaments.
11 Bocquet
12 Boitel—Gilding.
13 Bonnuit—Gilding, painting.
14 Boullemier, A.—Gilding.
15 Boullemier—Gilding.
16 Boullemier, son—Gilding.
17 Brecy—Ornaments.
18 Brunet-Rocques—Figures, scenes.

19 Cabau—Flowers.
20 Capronnier—Gilding.
21 Celos—Ornaments, modelling.
22 Charpentier—Gilding, painting.
23 Charrin, Mlle.—Portraits, scenes.
24 Constans—Gilding.
25 Constantin—Figures.
26 Courcy—Figures.
27 Coursajet—Gilder.
28 Dammouse—Ornaments, figures.
29 David—Gilding.
30 Davignon—Figures, scenes.
31 Delafosse—Figures.
32 Derichweiler—Painting.
33 Desperais—Ornaments.
34 Deutsch—Ornaments, gilding.
35 Develly—Figures, scenes.
36 Devicq—Screens, figures.
37 Didier—Ornaments.

FRANCE

Sèvres (Cont'd)

1 Doat—Decorator.
2 Doré—Ornaments.
3 Drouet—Gilding, flowers.
4 Drouet, E.—Figures, scenes.
5 Ducluseau, Mde.—Scenes, figures, portraits.
6 Durosey—Gilding.
7 Eaubonne, D'—Decorator.
8 Escallier, Mde.—Birds, animals, flowers.
9 Faraguet. Mde.—Scenes.
10 Ficquenet—Flowers and ornaments.
11 Fontaine—Flowers.
12 Fournier—Painting.
13 Fragonard—Figures, scenes.
14 Froment—Figures, scenes.
15 Ganeau—Gilding.
16 Gebleux—Ornaments.
17 Gely—Ornaments.
18 Georget—Portraits, scenes.
19 Gobert—Figures.
20 Goddé—Enamelling, gilding.
21 Godin, Mde.—Gilding.
22 Goupil—Scenes.
23 Guillemain
24 Hallion, E.—Landscapes.
25 Hallion, F.—Gilding.
26 Huard—Ornaments, medallions.
27 Humbert—Figure painter.
28 Jacobber—Flowers, fruit.
29 Jacquotot. Mde.—Groups, figures.
30 Jardel
31 Julienne—Ornaments.
32 Knipp, Mde.—Birds, animals, flowers.
33 Lambert—Ornaments, flowers.
34 Langlacé—Scenes, landscapes.
35 Langlois—Scenes, landscapes.
36 Lassere—Painting.

FRANCE

FRANCE

Sèvres (Cont'd)

1 Richard, F.—Decorator.
2 Richard, N.—Decorator.
3 Richard, L.—Painting.
4 Richard, P.—Decorative gilding.
5 Riocreux, I.—Pastorals, landscapes.
6 Riocreux, D.—Flowers.
7 Robert, P.—Scenes.
8 Robert, Mde.—Flowers, landscapes.
9 Robert, J.—Scenes.
10 Roger—Modelling.
11 Roussel—Figures.
12 Sandoz—Sculptor.
13 Schilt, F.—Portraits, figures.
14 Schilt, L.—Flowers.
15 Sieffert—Scenes, figures.
16 Simard—Decorator.
17 Sinsson—Flowers.
18 Solon—Figures, ornaments.
    1857-70.

19 Swebach—Scenes, figures.
20 Trager, J.—Birds, flowers.
21 Trager, H.—Painting.
22 Trager, L.—Painting.
23 Tristan—Gilding, painting.
24 Troyon—Ornaments.
25 Ulrich
26 Vignot—Ornaments.
27 Walter—Flowers.
28 Werdinger—Gilding.

Sinceny (1-11)
Established 1733.
1 About 1745.
2 About 1713. Pelleve.
3 After 1775.
4 A. Daussy.
5 Pierre Bertrand.
6 19th century factory.
7-11 Early marks.

FRANCE

Strasbourg (12-31)

1709-1780. Fayence and porcelain. The marks of a factory founded at Haguenau in 1724 are the same.

12-31 Marks of the Hannong family. Either incised, over, or under the glaze. 31 used on early pottery. Marks in blue, brown, and rose.

Tavernes (32-34)

1760-1780. Fayence.

32-34 M. Gaze.

Toulouse (35-36)

Fayence manufactory established early 18th century.

35 Early mark.

36 Fouque, Arnoux & Co. From 1820. Fayence and porcelain.

Tours (37-40)

Established 1842. Reproductions of Palissy ware. N. Sailly had a factory here in the 18th century.

37 Charles Avisseau, founder.

38, 39

40 F. M. Landais.

Uzes (41)

Francois Pichon. Fayence.

41 1st half 19th century.

Valenciennes (42-46)

Fayence factory founded about 1735. Porcelain factory here 1785 to 1798.

42-44 Dorez. Until 1748.

45, 46 On porcelain.

Varages (47-50)

Founded before 1740. Fayence.

47, 48

49 18th century mark in black, blue, or red.

50 Varages?

Vaux (51)

Established 1770. There is some confusion between this factory and Bordeaux.

51

Val-sous-meudon (52)

Metenhoff & Mourot.

52

Vincennes (53-62)

Fayence from 1767 to 1771. Soft paste porcelain factory established in 1745.

53, 54 Pierre Hannong. 1767-1771.

55, 56 Louis Philippe.

FRANCE

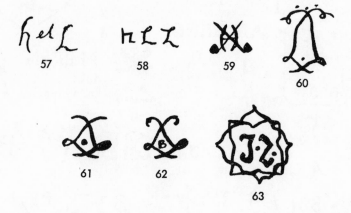

57   58   59   60

61   62   63

Vincennes (Cont'd)

Manufactory removed to Sèvres in 1756.
(See Sèvres). From 1767 to 1788
hard paste porcelain was manufactured at this place.

57, 58 Hannong & Lemaire. Porcelain.
59 Hannong.
60, 61 Before 1753.
62 1754. The letter "A" within the
"double L" denotes 1753, "B" denotes 1754, etc. Beware of copies of
these early marks.

Voisinlieu (63)

1839-1856. Fayence.
63 Ziegler.

GERMANY

Aich (1-3)
Porcelain. From 1849.
1 Impressed.
2, 3 Artists' initials.

Alt Haldensleben (4)
Factory of hard paste porcelain. M. Nathusius.
4 Mark stamped in blue.

Altrohlau (5-9)
Both pottery and porcelain. Established 1813.
5, 6 A. Nowotny. Impressed and in blue.
7-9

Amberg(10)
Late 19th century.
10

Annaburg (11)
Established 1874.
11 A. Heckmann.

Anspach (12-18)
Porcelain factory founded about 1758-1759.
12 Signature on early fayence.
13-18 On porcelain.

Arnstadt (20)
Established about 1808.
20

Aussig (21)
Established about 1840.
21 Joh Maresch.

Baden (22, 23)
1753-1778. A 19th century mark on fayence is BADEN impressed with a shield.
22, 23 In gold.

Bayreuth (24-32)
Fayence
24, 28 Pfeiffer (1760-1767 ?)
25, 26, 27, 29 Knöller (1720-1745)
30 Fränkel & Schrockh (1745-1751)
The weight of authority holds that no porcelain manufactory ever existed at Bayreuth in the 18th century. Some skillful decorators (*Hausmaler*) painted on Meissen porcelain at that time. **31** is attributed to the Bayreuth workshop of J. F. Metzsch.

Benedikt Bros. (33, 34)
Established 1884.
33, 34

Berlin (35-47)
Wegely period. Private factory. 1751-1757.
Gotzkowsky period. Private factory. 1761-63.
Royal factory. From 1763.
35-37 Wegely. Mark accompanied by impressed numbers.
38. Gotzkowsky.
39, 40, 41 Royal factory. 18th century from 1763. Mark in underglaze blue.

GERMANY

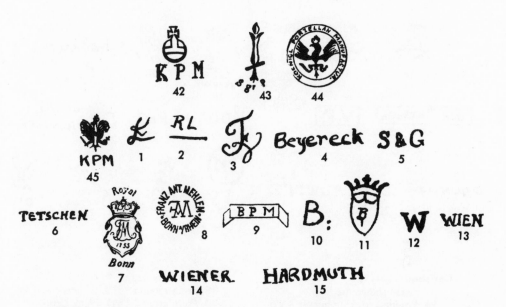

Berlin (Cont'd)
42 From 1832 Königliche Porzellan Manufaktur.
43 From 1882.
44 1847-1849.
45 1823-1832; 1844-1847.
Bernburg (1-3)
Fayence from about 1725.
1-3
Beyereck (4)
From about 1824.
4 Impressed on stoneware.
Bodenbach (5, 6)
From 1829.
5, 6 Schiller & Gerbing.

Bonn (7, 8)
Established by Clemens August.
7 2nd half 18th century.
8
Buckauer (9)
Buckauer Porzellan Manufactur.
9 Late mark.
Budau (10, 11)
Pottery made here in 19th century.
10 About 1825 under glaze.
11 About 1880. Impressed.
Budweis (12-15)
From about 1820. Porcelain.
12-15

GERMANY

Carlsbad (16-19)
All marks shown are late.
16 Products for Hamburger & Co.
17 C. L. Dwenger.
18, 19 Bawo & Dotter.

Charlottenberg (20)
20 Before 1830. The initials BPM and TPM are occasionally used with the eagle.

Chodau (21-26)
Established about 1804.
21-26

Dallwitz (27-30)
Established about 1804. Later marks than those given have two "L"s in the name.

27, 28 Early marks.
29 From around 1832. Lorenz.
30 From around 1845. Franz Urfus.

Damm (31)
Fayence. Established 1827.
31 From 1830 on figures reproduced from models acquired from defunct Höchst factory."

Danzig (32)
32

Dirmstein (33)
Existed until 1788. Fayence.
33

Dornheim (34)
34 Kock & Fischer.

GERMANY

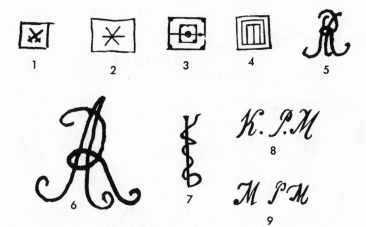

1
2
3
4
5
6
7
8 *K. P. M*
9 *M P M*

DRESDEN (Meissen) 1-40

First European hard paste porcelain manufactory established at Meissen, near Dresden, in 1710. Under-glaze crossed swords mark used with variations from about 1724 to present day. In 18th century, on figures the mark was painted on the (usually unglazed) base. In many cases it has disappeared in the firing. Often on figures of that period, the mark appears underglaze and very small at the back of the base. On modern Meissen figure reproductions the mark is generally underglaze with cursive incised letters and/or numbers. Unglazed bases appear occasionally on modern Meissen reproductions and marks are on unglazed base.

1, 2 Böttger's red stoneware. 1710-20 and later.

3, 4 Pseudo-Chinese marks about 1720-23.

5, 6 1725-1740. Under-glaze blue. On pieces intended (but not necessarily used) for the royal palaces or as royal gifts.
Generally decorated with oriental motifs.

7 1723 to about 1735. Found occasionally with crossed swords.

8 Königliche Porzellan Manufaktur (Royal Porcelain Manufacture). Under-glaze blue. 1723-24. Found only on tea-pots, stands and sugar-boxes. This mark is widely counterfeited.

9 Meissner Porzellan Manufaktur. Very early mark. Probably used about same time, or possibly earlier, than K. P. M. Rare.

GERMANY

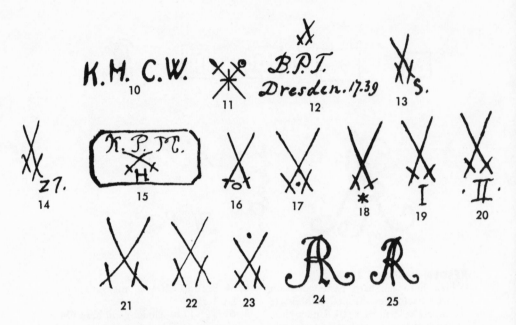

Dresden (1-40) (Cont'd)

10 K. H. C. W. Königliche Hof-Conditorei Warschau (Royal Court Store-room or Pantry Warsaw). Palace mark. Other similar palace marks used in the 18th century.

11 About 1725

12 Only a few pieces are known with this unexplained mark. Perhaps a palace mark or a mark on a service begun to order but never finished. It is found on spurious pieces made in modern times.

13, 14 1745-50.

15 1724. Very rare.

16, 17 1763-1774. Called "King's Period", "Dot Period" and "Academic Period".

18 Marcolini Period. 1774-1814.

19 1814-1818.

20 About 1818.

21, 22 1818-1924. Usually carefully drawn and generally with pommels in later period.

23 From 1924. Usually carefully drawn.

24, 25 Helene Wolfsohn. From about 1860. This was a porcelain decorating workshop. No porcelain was manufactured here. Appears on cups and saucers and parts of services as well as other wares. The authentic AR mark rarely appears on cups and saucers. No connection with Royal factory.

GERMANY

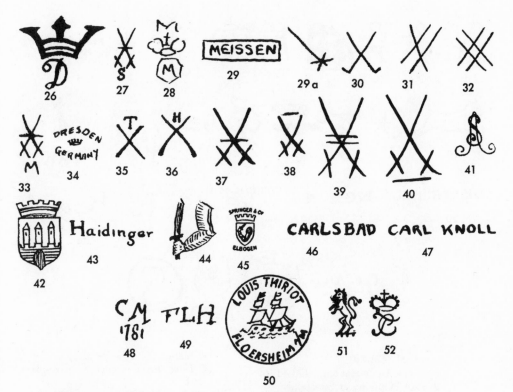

Dresden
26 Later Wolfsohn mark. "Crown Dresden". From about 1880.
27 Samson of Paris. Arch-imitator of Meissen and other great factories.
28 Muller at Coburg.
29, 29a, 30 Late marks of small factories, 29 impressed. 29a in blue.
31 Sitzendorf.
32 Coburg.
33 Meyers & Sohn.
34 Late mark of small manufactory.
35 Carl Thieme at Potschappel. Late 19th century.
36 Hirsch.
37 Meissen. The single nick cut across the mark was used on pieces sold undecorated out of the factory.
38-40 Meissen. Defective porcelain. As many as three or four nicks are sometimes found.

Eisenach (41)
Factory founded in 1858.
41 A. Saeltzer.

Eisenberger (42)
42

Elbogen (43, 44)
Established 1815. Porcelain.
43, 44 Early marks. Impressed.
45 Late mark. Springer & Co.

Fischern (46, 47)
Established 1848. Porcelain.
46, 47

Flörsheim (48-50)
Fayence around 1800.
48, 49 Christoph Mackenhauer.
50 After 1880.

Frankenthal (51, 52) (1-5)
Established 1755 by Paul Hannong. Closed 1800.
51 Paul Hannong. 1755-59.
Usually with initials P.H.. or initials without lion. Also, Joseph Anton Hannong, 1759-1762, with his monogram.
52 Administration of Elector Carl Theodore, 1762-1795

GERMANY

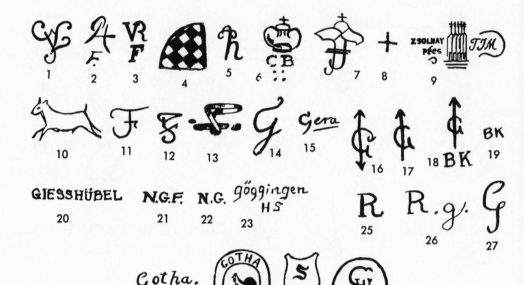

Frankenthal (Cont'd)
1 Joseph Anton Hannong. 1759-1762.
2 Paul Hannong at Strasbourg.
3 Van Recum. 1795-1799.
4 This mark also attributed to Nymphenburg. Paul Hannong.
5 Paul Hannong at Strasbourg.
Friedberg (6)
Fayence from 1754.
6 Chur Bayera.
Fulda (7, 8)
Established 1765. Closed 1790.
7, 8 Under-glaze in blue.
Fünfkirchen, Hungary (9)
Established in 1855.
9 W. Zsolnay. Mark in blue.
Fürstenberg (10-13)
Founded 1750. Porcelain.
10 Mostly on biscuit porcelain.
11, 12 Blue underglaze—often reproduced.
13 Modern factory mark.
Gera (14,15)
Established in 1779.

14 Mark in blue under glaze.
15 Later mark. Generally over-glaze red.
Giesshubel (16-22)
Established 1803. Porcelain.
16, 17 Early marks.
18, 19 From 1815.
20-22 From about 1845.
Göggingen (23)
Fayence factory established around 1750.
23 18th century mark.
Gotha (25-30)
Established around 1760.
25 Before 1795. Rotberg.
26 After 1790.
27 After 1805.
28 After 1805.
29 After 1880.
30 Simson Bros. From 1881.
Gräfenroda (31)
Fayence.
31 19th century mark. A. Schneider.

GERMANY

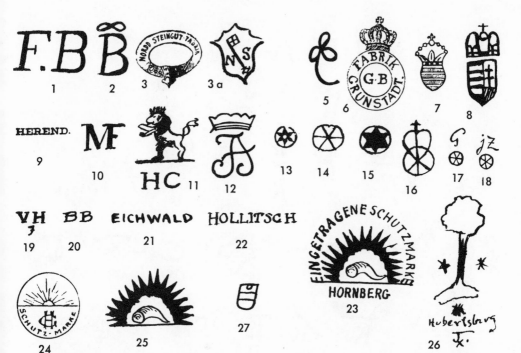

Greinstadt (1, 2)
Established 1800. Formerly Franken-thal.
1 Franz Bartolo. Since 1850.
2 Probably before 1850.

Grohn (3, 3A)
Fayence factory established 1870.
3, 3A

Grossbreitenbach (5)
Porcelain factory established about 1777.
5 Identical with Limbach .

Grunstadt (6)
Fayence.
6 After 1850.

Herend, Hungary (7-10)
7-10 From 1839. Moritz Fischer .

Hesse-Cassel (11)
Porcelain factory 1766-1788.
11 Lion or HC in underglaze blue.

Hildescheim (15)

Höchst (13-18)
Fayence 1746-1760.
13-18 Overglaze blue, red or gold.
Porcelain 1746-1796.

14, 17, 18 With or without letters which are probably painters' marks. To about 1770, with or without an Electoral hat above wheel. Sometimes impressed or overglaze black, brown, purple, iron-red and gold. From 1770 almost exclusively in underglaze blue. Generally no mark in biscuit.

Hohenstein (19-21)
Majolica from about 1850.
19, 20
21 From 1869.

Hollitsch, Hungary (22)
1743-1827. Majolica.
22 Mark impressed. 1786-1827.

Hornberg (23-25)
Fayence. Late 19th century.
23-25 Horn Bros.

Hubertsberg (26)
Late 18th century pottery.

Hutschendreuther, C.M. (27)
Founded 1814.
27 Mark under glaze in blue found on Vienna type ware.

GERMANY

Ilmenau (1-5)
From 1777. Imitation Wedgwood plaques, etc.
1 Same as Limbach
2, 3 Late 18th century.
4 From 1799. Nonne & Rosch.
5 Mid 19th century.

Kellinghusen (6-8)
1765-1840. Fayence.
6-8 Various potters marks.

Kelsterbach (Hesse-Darmstadt) (9)
1758-1769. Opened again in 1789.
9

Kiel (10-16)
Existed in 1764. Fayence.
10-12 1764-1768. Johann Taenich.
13-16 From 1768. J. Buchwald.

Klentsch (17)
Porcelain. From about 1835.
17

Kloster Veilsdorf (also Closter Veilsdorf) (18-22)
Porcelain factory established 1765.
18-22

Klosterle (23-28)
From 1793. Porcelain.
23-28

GERMANY

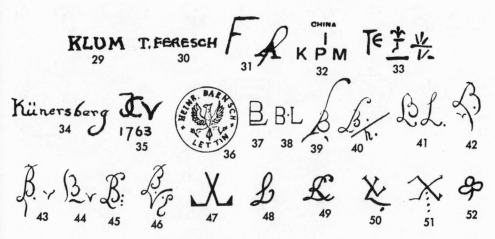

Klum (29-30)
Porcelain. 1st half 19th century.
29-30
Königstedten (31)
Fayence.
31 J. C. Frede
KPM (See Berlin)
Krister, C. (32)
32 On imitation Royal Berlin
Künersberg (33, 34)
Fayence.
33, 34
Lesum (35)
Fayence 1755-94.
35 Vielstick.
Lettin (36)
Established 1858.
36 Baensch.
Limbach (37-52) (1-7)
Established 1772. Porcelain.
37-51 Early marks. In red, black or
purple.
52 After 1797.

GERMANY

Limbach (Cont'd)
1-7 Early marks.

Ludwigsburg, Louisburg, or Kronenburg (8-16)
Established 1758. Factory closed in 1824. Ludwigsburg marks are often confused with Niderviller.
8-11 Probably the double "C" was used to 1806. In underglaze blue or over-glaze red (rare).
12 1793-1795.
13 1806-1816.
14 From 1816 to 1824. In gold.
15 1800-1810.
16 1770-1775.

Luftelburg (17)
17 Late mark.

Luxembourg (18-21)
Fayence factory established 1767; however, most of the wares found are late 19th century.
18, 19 Early marks.
20, 21 19th century.

Magdeburg-Neustadt (22)
Established 1865.
22 A. Bauer.

Marseille Armand (23)
Founded 1865.
23

Meissen (See Dresden)

GERMANY

Mettlach (24-44)
> Fayence factory originally founded in Luxembourg in 1767. Now operates at Mettlach.
> **24-44** 19th century marks.

Minden (45, 46)
> 18th century fayence factory.
> **45**
> **46** Coat of arms of the owners, the Hanstein family.

Miskolez (47)
> Established 1882.
> **47** Max Koos.

GERMANY

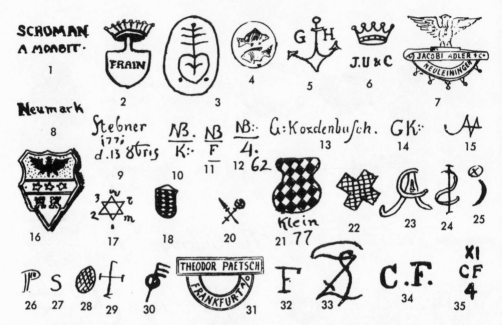

Moabit (1)
Porcelain. Established 1835 by M. Schuman.
1 Mark in blue generally with an eagle within a circle.

Moravia (2)
2 Frain.

Neufriedstein (3)
Fayence.
3 19th century mark.

Neuhaldensleben (4-6)
Marks found on mid 19th century copies of old majolica.
4 Mark impressed. H. Lonitz.
5 Hubbe Bros. Established 1875.
6 J. Uffrecht & Co.

Neuleiningen (7)
7 Jacobi Adler & Co. Established 1874.

Neumark (8)
Porcelain. About 1835.
8 Impressed.

Nuremberg (9-16)
Majolica factory established in 16th century.
9-15 Initials and names of various early potters.

Nymphenburg (17-29)
16 J. von Schwartz. Established 1880.
Porcelain factory founded 1747. Marks generally impressed. Factory first at Neudeck. Moved to Nymphenburg in 1761.
17 1753-61. Mark in blue.
18 Mark impressed.
20-29 Marks impressed or incised except when they are painters' marks.

Offenbach (30)
Fayence. Mid 18th century.
30

Paetsch, Theodor (31-32)
Factory at Frankfort.
31 Late mark. Paetsch.
32 Early Frankfort mark. 1661-1780.

Pfalz-Zweibrücken (33)
Porcelain factory established in 1767. Closed in 1775.
33 Mark in underglaze blue.

Pirkenhammer (34, 35) (1-6)
Hard paste porcelain factory established in 1802.
34, 35 Christian Fischer. From 1818. Mark stamped under glaze.

GERMANY

Pirkenhammer (Cont'd) (1-6)
    1-3 Fischer & Reichembach. Impressed.
    4-6 Fischer & Mieg. Mid 19th century.
Poppelsdorf (7, 7A)
    Fayence and porcelain. M. L. Wessel.
    7, 7A Mark stamped.
Prague (8-15)
    19th century porcelain factory established by Prager. Kriegel & Co. were successors.
    8-14
    15 Kriegel & Co.

Proskau (16-19)
    Fayence factory established 1763.
    16 1763-1770.
    17 1770-1783. Mark in brown or grey-blue.
    18 After 1783.
    19 Stamped on early 19th century brownware.
Rauenstein (20-24)
    Porcelain factory established about 1780. Marks in blue, red, purple and black.
    20, 21 Earliest marks.
    22 Probably before 1800.
    23, 24 After 1800.

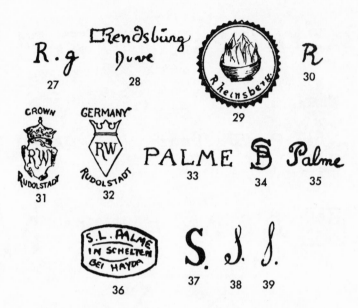

Regensburg (27)

18th century earthenware factory. Porcelain was made in 19th century.

27 This mark also attributed to Gotha.

Rendsburg (28)

Fayence. 1765-1818.

28

Rheinsberg (29)

Fayence factory established 1815.

29 F. Hildebrandt.

Rückingen (30)

Fayence factory here.

Rudolstadt (31, 32)

It has not been definitely established that there ever was any but a modern factory at Rudolstadt. (See Volkstedt).

31, 32 Late 19th century marks. Impressed or stamped.

Schelten (33-36)

Pottery factory founded 1820.

33-36 Marks impressed or stamped. S. L. Palme.

Schlaggenwald (37-39)

Porcelain factory established in early 19th century.

37-39 Early marks incised, black, blue, red or gold.

GERMANY

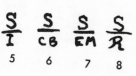 

 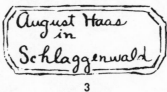 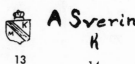

Schlaggenwald (Cont'd) (1-4)
   1, 2 Lippert & Haas. Circa 1840.
   3, 4
Schleswig (5-8)
   Fayence from mid 18th century.
   5-8
Schlierbach (9)
   Established about 1831.
   9
Schlierwald (10)
   Late 19th century porcelain factory.
   10 In blue.
Schretzheim or Scherzheim (11, 12)
   Fayence factory 1752-1872.
   11, 12 On fayence
Schweidnitz (13)
   Fayence factory established 1882.
   13 M. Krause
Schwerin (14)
   Fayence factory here from about 1760.
   14 Appelstadt.

GERMANY

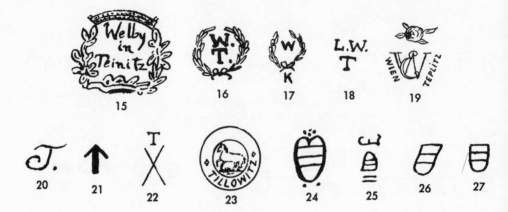

Teinitz (15-18)
   15-18 F. L. Welby. Mark impressed or stamped.
Teplitz (19)
   19th century factory. Frilly figures, vases, etc.
   19 E. Wien. There are other marks, most of which incorporate this name.
Tettau (20)
   20
Thieme, Carl (21, 22)
   Established at Potschappel in latter half of 19th century.
   21, 22 In blue.
Tillowitz (23)
   23 19th century.
Vienna (24-27)
   Porcelain factory established 1718 by DuPaquier. Pieces never marked during DuPaquier Period (1718-1744). In 1744 it became a state manufactory and adopted the Austrian shield as a mark.

24-27 The *Bindenschild* mark from 1744-1749 was painted as a rule in iron-red, purple or black but sometimes also impressed or incised in the paste in more or less irregular form. From 1749-1827, the mark was painted in underglaze blue for the first thirty or forty years somewhat slantways, rather large and in thick strokes. Between 1770 and 1810 it became smaller, and rounded in shape. After that, for a long time it was long and narrow and in the 1820's it was almost triangular. In 1827, the blue mark was superseded by an uncolored impressed mark of more regular shape. The last two numerals of the year were often impressed from 1783. The last three after 1800. The factory closed in 1864. Since then many modern reproductions with similar marks have appeared on the market.

GERMANY

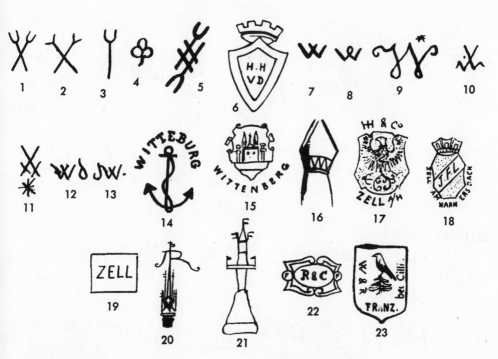

Volkstedt (1-5)
Established 1760 by George Macheleid. Another late 19th century factory copied all of the "hayfork" marks.
1, 2 1760-1787.
3 1787-1799.
4 From about 1790.
5 Mark on late 19th century pieces.

Vordamm (6)
Fayence factory established 1840.
6 A. Franke.

Wallendorf (7-11)
Porcelain factory established by Hammann in 1762. Marks generally painted in blue.
7-10
11 This mark used until protest from Meissen factory.

Wiesbaden (12, 13)
12, 13 1770-1795.

Witteburg (14)
Fayence manufactory here in 19th century.
14

Wittenberger (15)
Established 1884.
15

Würzburg (16)
Founded in 1775 by Johann Geyger. Porcelain.
16

Zell (17-19)
Fayence works established about 1820 by F. Lenz.
17 Haager, Horth & Co. About 1850.
18, 19 Carl Schaaf. Before 1850. **19** Impressed.

Znaim (20, 21)
Majolica factory founded 1835.
20 Klammerth. 19th century.
21 S. Pepovecki.

Misc. 19th-20th century German marks; (22, 23) (1-60) (1-27)
Reissberger & Co. **(22)**. Established 1882.
22
Rissler & Co. **(23)**. Established in Freiburg in 1847.
23

GERMANY

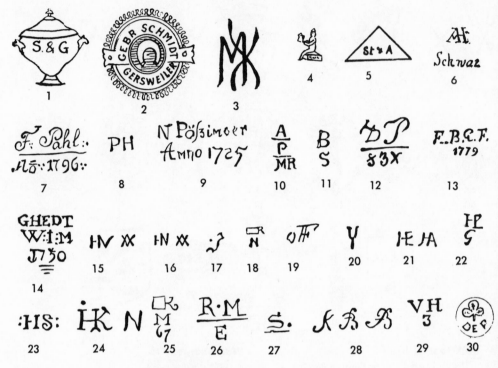

Miscellaneous German Marks (1-60)
(Cont'd)
Schemlzer & Gericke (1)
   Established 1865.
1
Schmidt Brothers (2, 3)
   Established 1847.
2, 3

Schmidt, H. (4)
   Established 1842.
4
Steiner & Adler (5)
   Established 1889.
5
6 From 1801.

GERMANY

Miscellaneous German Marks (1-60)
(Cont'd)

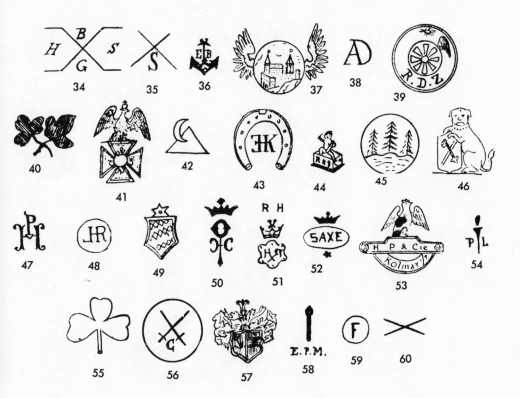

GERMANY

Miscellaneous German Marks (1-27)
(Cont'd)

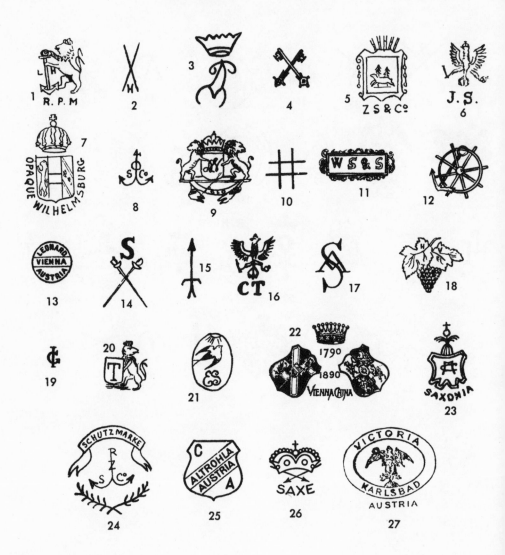

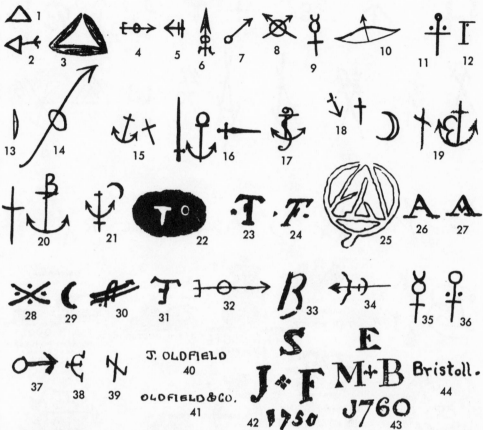

Bow (1-39)

Soft paste porcelain factory established in 1744. Transferred to Derby in 1776. Some of the marks given have been hesitantly attributed to Bow and a number of them are questionable. They are generally incised or painted in blue or red.

1-14

15-21 Painted in red and blue.

22 Monogram of Tebo? Impressed.

23, 24 Monogram of Thomas Frye?

25-30 Various workmen's marks.

31 Frye?

32-39

Brampton (40, 41)

Established in the 18th century. A few factories here in the 19th century pro-

ducing brown-ware.

40, 41 From 1826. Factory originally Oldfield, Madin, Wright, Hewitt & Co., est. 1810.

Bristol (42-44) (1-28)

Pottery made here in early 18th century, porcelain later in same century. Champion's porcelain factory established about 1770 under name, Wm. Cookworthy & Co. Formerly at Plymouth, the work is similar. Factory was sold about 1778. Marks are in red, blue, gold, etc.

42 Joseph Flower. From 1743. On Delft.

43 Michael Edkins. Painter on Delft.

44 About 1750. In relief.

GREAT BRITAIN

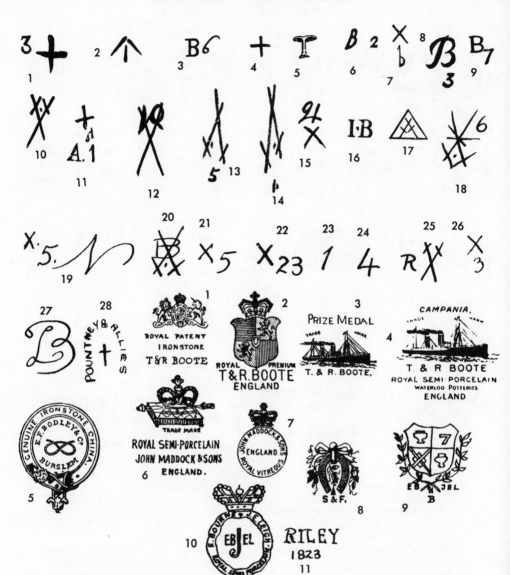

Bristol (Cont'd)

1-26 Usually painted in overglaze blue or gold.

27 On porcelain made by Count Brancas-Lauragais.

28 Pountney & Allies. From about 1820 to 1837. After 1837 it was Pountney & Gouldney.

Burslem (1-48)

Numerous manufactories here from 17th century. Most of the potters at Burslem produced earthenware.

1-4 T. & R. Boote. From 1850. 2 and 4 are late 19th century marks.

5 E. F. Bodley & Co. From about 1860.

6, 7 John Maddock & Sons. Marks from 1891.

8 Smith & Ford. Late 19th century.

9, 10 E. Bourne & J. E. Leigh. 19th century.

11 1814-1826. Impressed.

GREAT BRITAIN

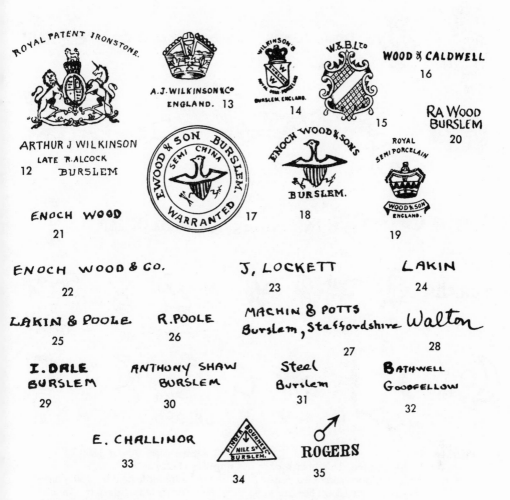

ROYAL PATENT IRONSTONE.

ARTHUR J WILKINSON
LATE R.ALCOCK
12   BURSLEM

A.J.WILKINSON&Co
ENGLAND. 13

14

W&B.Lᵗᵒ

15

WOOD & CALDWELL
16

RA WOOD
BURSLEM
20

E.WOOD & SON BURSLEM.
SEMI CHINA
WARRANTED   17

ENOCH WOOD & SONS
BURSLEM.
18

ROYAL
SEMI PORCELAIN

WOOD & SON
ENGLAND.
19

ENOCH WOOD
21

ENOCH WOOD & CO.
22

J, LOCKETT
23

LAKIN
24

LAKIN & POOLE
25

R. POOLE
26

MACHIN & POTTS
Burslem, Staffordshire
27

Walton
28

I. DALE
BURSLEM
29

ANTHONY SHAW
BURSLEM
30

Steel
Burslem
31

BATHWELL
GOODFELLOW
32

E. CHALLINOR
33

PINDER, BOURNE & C
NILE Sᵗ
BURSLEM.
34

ROGERS
35

Burslem (Cont'd)
12-14 A. J. Wilkinson. 13, 14 are late 19th century marks.
15 Wood & Barker, Ltd. Late 19th century factory.
16 Wood & Caldwell. 1790-1818.
17, 18 Enoch Wood & Sons. 1818-1846.
19 Wood & Son. Late 19th century.
20 Ralph Wood. Before 1797.
21, 22 Late 18th century marks.
23 About 1800.

24, 25 1770-1795.
26 From 1795.
27 About 1830.
28 John Walton. 1790-1839.
29 About 1800.
30 From 1850.
31 1766-1824.
32 An impressed mark used from 1800 to 1819.
33 From 1819.
34 19th century factory.
35 About 1790-1842.

GREAT BRITAIN

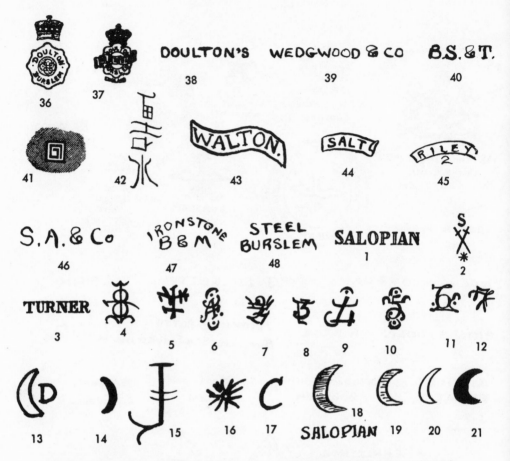

36-38 Royal Doulton. This branch of the Doulton factory succeeded Pinder & Bourne about 1880 (See Lambeth).

39 Ralph Wedgwood 1790-96

40 Barker, Sutton & Till. 1830-1850.

41, 42 John and David Elers. 1688 to about 1710.

43 John Walton. 1790 to about 1840. Mark impressed.

44 Ralph Salt. 1812 to about 1835. Mark impressed.

45 Riley (John and Richard). About 1800-26.

46 Smith, Ambrose & Co. About 1790.

47 Bagshaw & Maier. About 1800.

48 Daniel Steel. About 1800-24.

Caughley (1-25)

Earthenware made here in 1750. Porcelain factory established by Thomas Turner in 1772. Purchased in 1799 by John Rose & Co. of Coalport, and operated until 1814. The Willow pattern was produced from 1780.

1 Impressed. From about 1772.

2 Copy of a Meissen mark.

3-25 1772-1799. Many of these marks are similar to those of Worcester. Turner sent much undecorated porcelain to the Worcester factory for decoration. Most of these marks are printed or painted in blue underglaze.

GREAT BRITAIN

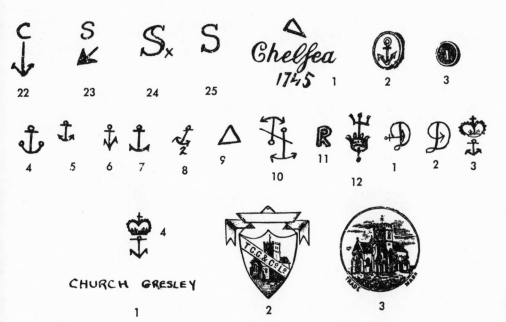

Caughley (Cont'd)
22-25
Chelsea (1-12)

Porcelain factory established about 1743. Sold to proprietor of Derby factory in 1770. Both factories were then operated jointly until 1784 when the factory was moved permanently to Derby.

1 An early mark. 1743 is earliest known.

2, 3 1749-1753. Anchor colorless or in red on raised oval medallion.

4, 5 1750-1758. Mark painted in red, brown or purple.

6, 7 1758-1770. Mark in gold, occasionally in red.

8 1743-1748. In red.

9 1743-1748. Incised.

10 In gold on fine pieces.

11

12 1743-1751. In blue under-glaze.

Chelsea-Derby period (1-4)

The Chelsea factory was operated jointly with Derby from 1770 to 1784 by Wm. Duesbury. 1784 saw its removal to Derby. The models were interchanged so the wares of this period have characteristics representative of both factories.

1-4 1770-1782. Marks overglaze in blue, puce, or, in gold.

Church Gresley (1-3)

Porcelain factory established 1794 and closed in 1808. Successful earthenware factory established about 1790. Henry Tooth and William Ault had a factory here from 1882 to 1886.

1 Impressed or scratched in the paste. 1794-1808.

2, 3 T. G. Green & Co. Founded 1790. These marks date in latter half 19th century.

GREAT BRITAIN

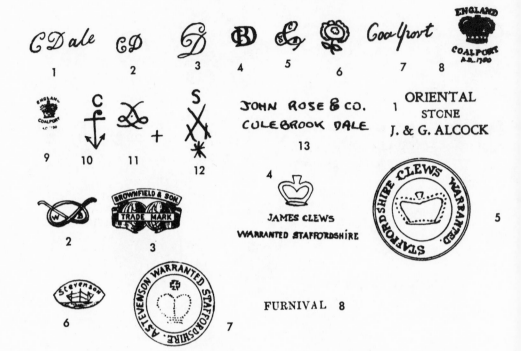

1   2   3   4   5   6   7   8

9   10   11   12

JOHN ROSE & CO.
CULEBROOK DALE
13

ORIENTAL
STONE
J. & G. ALCOCK   1

2   3

4

JAMES CLEWS
WARRANTED STAFFORDSHIRE

5

6   7

FURNIVAL 8

Coalport (1-13)

Porcelain manufactory established between 1780 and 1790 by John Rose. This firm bought up the Caughley Manufactory in 1799, Swansea in 1820, and Nantgarw in 1828. Many old pieces were unmarked.

1-3 Coalbrookdale. Marks used early in 19th century.

4 A little later than the above. Occasionally this mark is found encircled with the name, Daniell, London.

5 Used after 1828. The CSN stands for Caughley, Swansea, Nantgarw.

6, 7 Early 19th century mark.

8, 9 From 1891. This same mark without "England" was adopted about 10 years earlier.

10 Imitation of the Chelsea mark.

11 Imitation of the Sevres mark.

12 Imitation of a Meissen mark. (See Caughley, 2).

13 Coalbrookdale. From about 1850.

Cobridge (1-18)

A. Stevenson was working here before 1818. James Clews had a factory from 1818 to 1829. In 1836 W. Brownfield and others established works here. Other potters in 1843 include Francis Dillon. Elijah Jones, Stephen Hughes & Co., B. E. Godwin, J. M. and J. Godwin, John and Robert Godwin, G. and R. Leigh, and Coxon, Harding & Co. In 1900 there were the following: H. Alcock & Co., Banner & Co., Brownfield's Pottery, Ltd., Furnivals, Ltd., and Pidduck, Ruston & Co.

1 J. & G. Alcock at Cobridge in 1843.

2 W. Brownfield. 1850-1871.

3 After 1871. Brownfield.

4, 5 Until 1829. James Clews.

6, 7 Stevenson. Before 1818. Succeeded by Clews.

8 Furnivals, Ltd., established about 1850.

GREAT BRITAIN

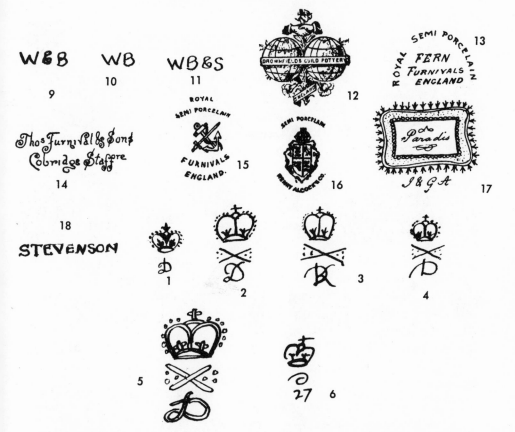

GREAT BRITAIN

Derby (Contd.)

7

8 Same as 6. The number shown is the pattern number.

9 Same as 6.

10 Incised on a few early pieces. (Butts, Rivett & Heath, 1745-50)?

11 Incised or in blue or red. 1765-1780.

12

13 Joseph Hills, an employee.

14 Isaac Farnsworth, an employee.

15-23 1815-1848. Robert Bloor operated the works from 1815, but the mark with his name was not generally used until 1825-30. 15 is the earliest Bloor mark. 17, 18, and 19 are from about 1830.

24-31 Various marks on early specimens of Derby.

32 1848-1859. Locker & Co.

33 From 1859. Stevenson, Sharp & Co.

Derby (Cont'd)

34 After 1848.

35 After 1859. Stevenson & Hancock until 1866. Then Sampson Hancock alone.

36 Crown Derby Porcelain Co. established 1875. The words "Royal Crown Derby" were incorporated as part of the mark in 1890. From about 1891 the word "England" was used in the mark.

37-41 Various marks used before 1815.

42-59 Miscellaneous marks. (Workmen, patterns, etc.)

Fenton District (1-24)

Many potteries in this area. Some date from early 18th century. Miles Mason established 1780. In 1851 Francis Morley purchased the Mason works and removed them to Shelton where they were bought by the Ashworths in 1859 and consequently moved to Hanley.

1 John Barker. 18th century mark.

2 Felix Pratt. 1775-1810.

3 Thomas Green. About 1830 to 1859.

4 S. Greenwood. 1770-1780.

5 F. and R. Pratt & Co. After 1810.

6 Crown Staffordshire Porcelain Co. From 1890.

GREAT BRITAIN

7

H & C
F

8

MILES

MASON

9

MASON'S CAMBRIAN   M. MASON
ARGIL

10

11

FENTON STONE WORKS
C. J. M. & Co.

12

MASON'S PATENT
IRONSTONE CHINA

13

MASON'S

PATENT IRONSTONE
CHINA

14

19

MASONS IRONSTONE
CHINA

ASHWORTHS   15

Real
IRONSTONE
CHINA

16

Carey's
Saxon Stone

17

ETRUSCAN
E K B

18

MYATT

WHIELDON

20

WARRANTED
IRONSTONE CHINA

TRADE MARK

JOHN EDWARDS.
ENGLAND.

21

PORCELAINE DE TERRE
TRADE MARK

JOHN EDWARDS
ENGLAND. 22

JE&S
Dale Hall
23

PEACOCK
POTTERY
24

DM

SANDS END
FULHAM

1

Fenton (Cont'd)

7 Crown Staffordshire Porcelain Co. This mark from 1906.

8 Hulme & Christie. 19th century mark.

9 Late 18th century. Stamped in clay.

10 Mark with name of pattern after 1813. Mason.

11 Late 18th century.

12 After 1805. Charles James Mason & Co.

13, 14 1813-1851. These marks in blue were used through the end of the 19th century by the Ashworths.

15 After 1859. Geo. L. Ashworth & Bros. These works at Hanley.

16 1851-1859. Ridgway, Morley, Wear & Co. This mark impressed with Royal Arms, crest, motto, etc. Factory at Shelton.

17 About 1845. Impressed.

18 First Elkin, Knight & Co., then Elkin, Knight & Bridgwood. About

1820-1850.

19 Joseph Myatt. About 1800.

20 Thomas Whieldon. About 1740 to 1798. Mark impressed.

21, 22 John Edwards. After 1891.

23 J. Edwards & Son 1842-1882.

24 Foley China Works. Established 1850. Now E. Brain & Co. This is a modern mark.

Fulham (1)

John Dwight made salt glazed stoneware here from about 1671-1703. The works were carried on until 1862 by various descendants. From 1862 to 1864 MacIntosh & Clements were owners. In 1864 C. T. Bailey purchased the works. A Wm. de Morgan after removing his works from Surrey had a factory in Fulham from 1888 to 1907.

1 Wm. de Morgan. 1888-1907. This mark was used without the address at Surrey from 1882 to 1888.

GREAT BRITAIN

1

2

3

4

5

6

H.P.

NEALE & PALMER 10

NEALE & WILSON 11

7

8

9

WILSON 12

J. VOYEZ
13

VOYEZ & HALES
14

Neale & Co.
15

E. Mayer 16

E. MAYER & SON
17

JOSEPH MAYER
18 & Co.

T., J. & J. MAYER
19

MAYER BROS.
20

T & J HOLLINS
21

Keeling Toft & Co.
22

Hanley District (1-45)

Many manufactories in this district. Geo. L. Ashworth & Bros. transferred the Mason Ironstone factory to Hanley in 1859. (See Fenton)

1 E. J. Bodley. Late 19th century.

2 Whittaker, Heath & Co. Late 19th century.

3 F. Winkle & Co. Late 19th century.

4 Upper Hanley Pottery Co. Late 19th century.

5 J. H. Wetherby & Sons. Late 19th century.

6 Sherwin & Cotton. Late 19th century.

7, 8 Humphrey Palmer. 1760-1776. Impressed.

9 Neale. About 1776. Impressed.

10 Neale & Palmer. 1776-1786.

11 Neale & Wilson. From 1786.

12 R. Wilson, then D. Wilson & Sons. 1787-1820.

13 J. Voyez. About 1780.

14 Voyez & Hales. About 1785.

15 Neale & Co. From 1776.

16 Elijah Mayer. From 1770 to 1813.

17 E. Mayer & Son. 1813-1830.

18 Joseph Mayer & Co. Early 19th century.

19, 20 Thomas, John and Joseph Mayer. From 1836.

21 T. and J. Hollins. About 1780-1820.

22 Keeling, Toft & Co. 1806-24. Succeeded by Toft & May.

GREAT BRITAIN

MEIGH	SHORTHOSE & HEATH	Shorthose & C.º
23	24	25

T. SNEYD	MANN & Co.	LAKIN & POOLE	Birch	E.J.B.
26	HANLEY	28	29	30
	27			

M.&N.	W. STEVENSON, HANLEY	HACKWOOD
31	32	33

Powell & Bishop
34

35

BEST P&B
36

P&B
37

38

39

40

C WILSON
41

DUDSON, ENGLAND
42

DUDSON BROTHERS
HANLEY, ENGLAND
43

J. H. WEATHERBY
& SONS
44

J.H.W. & SONS
HANLEY
ENGLAND
45

Hanley (Cont'd)

23 Meigh & Sons. From about 1780 well into 19th century. Impressed.

24 Shorthose & Heath. 1802-1826.

25 Shorthose & Co. 1783-1802. Mark in blue.

26 T. Sneyd. Mid 19th century.

27 Mann & Co. Mid 19th century.

28 Lakin & Poole. 1770-1794. Impressed.

29, 30 E. J. Birch. Late 18th century. Marks impressed.

31 Mayer & Newbold. 1823-37.

32 W. Stevenson. About 1828.

33 Hackwood. 1842-56.

34-37 Powell & Bishop. 1865-1878.

Marks impressed or printed. 35 generally has a seated figure under it.

38 Bishop & Stonier. Late 19th century.

39 J. & G. Meakin. After 1891.

40 J. Dimmock & Co. Late 19th century.

41 Robert Wilson. From about 1790. The name "Wilson" is sometimes omitted.

42. 43 Dudson Bros., successors to James T. Dudson. Works est. 1800. These marks after 1891.

44, 45 Modern firm. Later than 1891. J. H. Weatherby (Wetherby?) & Sons.

T. WETHERILL
1

Doulton & Watts
Lambeth Pottery
3

DOULTON
IMPASTO
4

STEPHEN
GREEN
Lambeth
2

DOULTON
LAMBETH
CARRARA
ENGLAND
5

DOULTON
SILICON
LAMBETH
ENGLAND
6

LAMBETH
12.7.
1880
DOULTON
& RIX'S
PATENT
MARQUETERIE-ENGLAND
7

DOULTON
& SLATER'S
PATENT
8

DOULTON
LAMBETH
ENGLAND.
9

DOULTON
LAMBETH
ENGLAND
10

DOULTON
LAMBETH·ENGLAND
11

LEEDS ★ POTTERY
1

LEEDS · POTTERY
LEEDS · POTTERY
2

GREEN,
LEEDS
3

L.P.
4

↗
5

✗
6

♔
G
7

C G
W
8

⫘⊶➔
9

C G
10

HARTLEY, GREENS & Co.
LEEDS POTTERY
11

R.B. & S.
12

D. D. & Co.
CASTLEFORD.
13

RAINFORTH & CO.
14

T.N. & Co
15

Lambeth (1-11)

Early potters here noted for English Delft. The Doulton factory has been carried on by members of the family since 1815. It is in operation today.

1 T. Wetherill. 19th century modeller.

2 Stephen Green. Impressed. About 1835.

3 Doulton and Watts. 1820-58. Founded in 1815 in Vauxhall.

4-11 Doulton. The marks in this group possessing the word "England" were used after 1891. When the words "Made in England" appear, the piece may be dated about 30 or fewer years ago.

Lane Delph

Information on the Mason works and other manufactories at this place is included under Fenton.

Leeds (1-15)

Pottery factory established about 1/60 by Green Brothers. Humble, Green & Co. was formed in 1775. In 1783 it was Hartley, Greens & Co. In 1825 the firm was absorbed by Samuel Wainwright & Co. The Leeds Pottery Co. were the owners in 1832. It changed hands again in 1840 when Stephen and James Chapel were the proprietors. Warburton, Britton & Co. operated it in 1850 before Richard Britton & Sons took control in 1863.

1-11 Early marks. (See above)

12 1863-1878. Richard Britton & Sons.

13 David Dunderdale & Co. 1790-1820. Castleford pottery.

14 About 1780. Rainforth & Co. Mark impressed.

15 From 1854. Thomas Nicholson & Co. Castleford.

GREAT BRITAIN

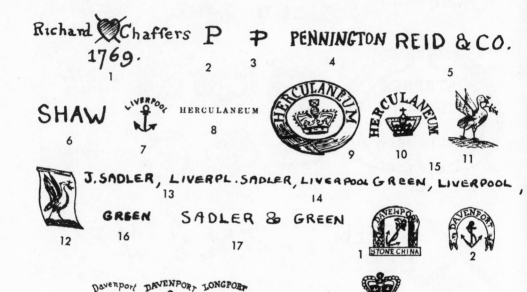

Liverpool (1-17)

Besides the potters mentioned, the following Liverpool men were noted for their 18th century wares: Philip Christian, Zachariah Barnes, Thomas Spencer, James Drinkwater, and Samuel Gilbody. Richard Abbey established himself in 1793. In 1796 his works were purchased by the Messrs. Worthington, Humble, & Holland and named Herculaneum Pottery. From 1833 to 1836 Case, Mort & Co. were the proprietors. The firm then became Mort & Simpson until 1841.

1 Richard Chaffers. Est. 1752.

2-4 Seth Pennington. 1760-1790. Marks in gold or colors.

5 W. Reid & Co. About 1754 to 1760.

6 Thomas Shaw. 1740-1770.

7 Herculaneum. 1796-1836.

8-10 Herculaneum. Until 1841. Impressed or printed.

11-12 Herculaneum. 1833-1841.

13, 14 John Sadler. About 1756-1770.

15, 16 Guy Green. Est. about 1756.

17 Sadler & Green. 1756 to about 1770. Green carried on from about 1770 to 1799.

Longport (1-12)

John Davenport established a porcelain factory in 1793. His sons Henry and William inherited it in 1848 and it prospered until 1887.

1-6 Davenport. After 1793. 1—printed. 2-5—Generally impressed. 6—In color.

7 After 1806. Davenport.

8 Later Davenport mark. Impressed.

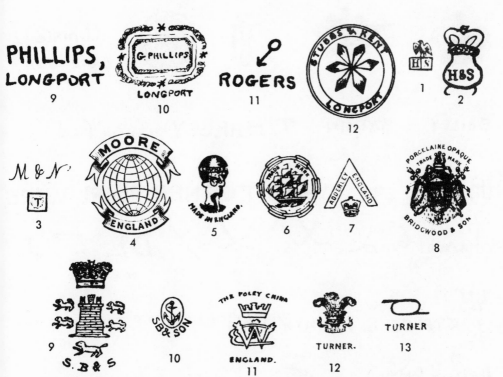

**PHILLIPS,
LONGPORT**
9

G. PHILLIPS
LONGPORT
10

ROGERS
11

STUBBS & KENT
LONGPORT
12

1

H&S
2

M & N
3

MOORE
ENGLAND
4

MADE IN ENGLAND
5

TRADE MARK
6

ADDERLEY ENGLAND
7

PORCELAINE OPAQUE
TRADE MARK
BRIDGWOOD & SON
8

S. B & S
9

SB & SON
10

THE FOLEY CHINA
W
ENGLAND.
11

TURNER.
12

TURNER
13

Longport (Cont'd)

9, 10 G. Phillips. About 1760 to about 1830.

11 Rogers. 1780-1829.

12 Stubbs & Kent. 1798-1829. This dating is questionable.

Longton (Lane End) (1-39)

Bankes and Turner established 1756 at Stoke. John Turner moved to Lane End in 1762. The firm of Abbott & Turner was formed. Turner died in 1786. His sons William and John carried on until 1803. Among manufactories here in 1900 were the following: C. Amison; Arrowsmith & Co.; G. L. Bentley & Co.; Beresford Bros.; J. H. Beswick; Blair & Co.; Boulton & Co.; F. Cartlidge & Co.; Collingwood Bros.; J. Cope & Co.; Dresden Porcelain Co.; Hammersley & Co.; Hill & Co.; J. W. Holt; Long-ton Porcelain Co.; McNeal & Co.; Moore Bros.; G. Proctor & Co.; Redfern & Drakeford; Robinson & Son; Rowley & Newton, Ltd.; J. Shore & Co.; Sampson Smith; Stone China Co.; Taylor & Kent; Joseph Unwin & Co.; T. Walters; G. Warrilow & Sons; Wildblood, Heath & Sons; T. Wild & Co.; Wileman & Co.; H. M. Williamson & Sons; and J. B. Wood & Co.

1, 2 Hilditch & Son. Est. about 1830. Succeeded by Hilditch & Hopwood.

3 Mayer & Newbold. 1800-1837.

4 Moore Bros. Late 19th century.

5 D. Chapman. 20th century mark.

6, 7 Wm. Adderley & Co. From 1870.

8-10 Sampson, Bridgwood & Son. Late 19th century.

11 Wileman & Co.

12, 13 John Turner. From 1872.

GREAT BRITAIN

14   15   16   17   18

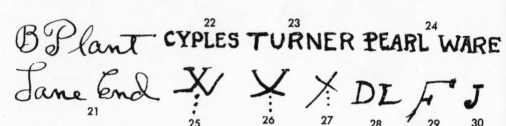

BAILEY & BATKIN
19

20
T. HARLEY Lane End

22   23   24
B Plant CYPLES TURNER PEARL WARE

Lane End   X   X   X   DL   F   J
21   25   26   27   28   29   30

32   33   34
31 **CYPLES & BARKER** J&G LOCKETT J.LOCKETT & SONS

35
Bailey & Batkin

      CHAS ALLERTON & SONS
REGINA   ENGLAND
H.& G.   38
39   1   36   37

Longton (Cont'd)

14, 15 R. H. Plant & Co. Late 19th century.

16, 17 J. Holdcroft.

18 John Aynsley. 1790-1826.

19 Bailey & Batkin. Circa 1815.

20 T. Harley. Earthenware factory about 1810.

21 Benj. Plant. About 1790.

22 Cyples. About 1786.

23 John Turner. From 1762. Mark impressed.

24 Chetham & Wooley. About 1800.

25-27 William Littler. About 1750 to about 1758. Soft paste porcelain.

28-31 Marks also attributed to Littler. 30—in blue.

32 Cyples & Barker. Circa 1800.

33 J. & G. Lockett. From 1802.

34 J. Lockett & Sons. From 1829.

35 Bailey & Batkin. Impressed. From about 1800.

36 James Kent. Modern mark.

37, 38 Chas. Allerton. Est. 1831. These marks after 1891.

39 Holland & Green. From 1853.

Lowesby (1)

Earthenware factory here.

1 F. G. Fowke. Established about 1835. Mark impressed or stamped. Occasionally only the name is used.

GREAT BRITAIN

Lowestoft (1-28)

Soft paste porcelain factory here from 1757 to 1802. The "Armorial" china attributed to Lowestoft was made in China. There is no regular factory mark. Some Chinese symbols were used. Some Lowestoft was sent from China plain for decoration in England.

1-28 Lowestoft. The numerals are generally found inside the rim on the bottom of the specimen. Many of these workmen's marks were painted in blue.

Middlesborough (1, 2)

Earthenware factory here around 1845.

1 Impressed.

2 About 1845. Stamped.

Mortlake (1, 2)

Pottery founded about 1750 by William Sanders. Joseph Kishere was operating a stoneware factory here in 1811.

1, 2 Joseph Kishere. Around 1811. Mark impressed.

Nantgarw, Wales (1, 3)

Founded in 1811 by Billingsley of the Worcester factory. It closed for about 3 years in 1814 when the workers went to the Swansea works. In 1816 it reopened. Billingsley left again for Coalport in 1819 and the factory was carried on by Wm. Young & Thos. Pardoe until Oct. 1822. It was again opened by the Pardoes 10 years later.

1 Nantgarw China Works. Impressed. Sometimes painted, stencilled, or transfer printed in red, gold and other colors.

2 In red.

3 Impressed.

Newcastle-on-Tyne (1-6)

Newcastle and Sunderland are closely associated.

1, 2 Sewell & Donkin. Pottery. Around 1780. Marks impressed.

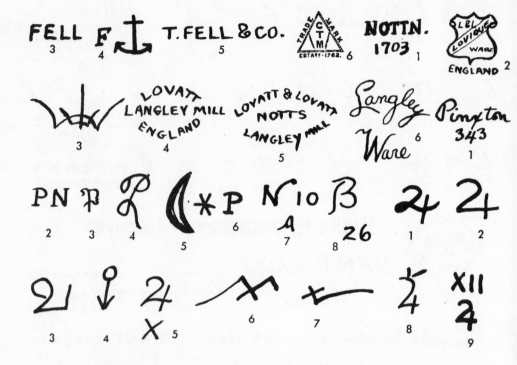

Newcastle (Cont'd)

3, 4, 5 From 1817. Thomas Fell & Co. Marks impressed.

6 T. Malling & Sons. Late 19th century mark.

Nottingham (1-6)

Stoneware was made here as early as 1693. Little of it was marked. Inscriptions with names and dates are found on some pieces.

1 1703. Pottery.

2-6 Lovatt & Lovatt. Late 19th and early 20th century.

Pinxton (1-8)

Soft paste porcelain factory established by Wm. Billingsley and John Coke, 1796-1813. The porcelain was generally unmarked. The factory closed 1813.

1 About 1793-1812.

2-4 About 1793-1812.

5 About 1793-1812. Mark in puce.

6 About 1793-1812. Mark impressed.

7 About 1793-1812. Mark in red.

8 About 1793-1812. If this is Billingsley's initial, then 1796-1801.

Plymouth (1-11)

Porcelain factory established here by William Cookworthy about 1755. The factory was moved to Bristol in 1770 and sold to Richard Champion in 1773. Some Bristol marks are similar to those of Plymouth.

1-9 About 1755-1770. These Plymouth marks in red, painted or enamelled in blue or in gold.

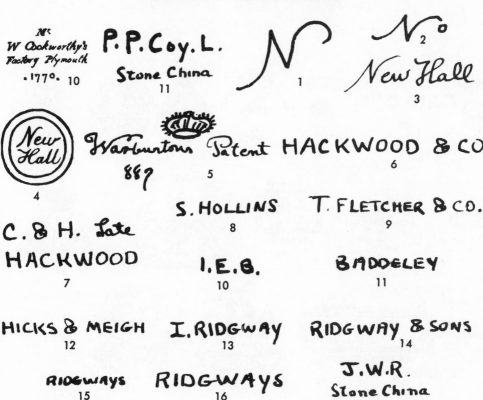

Plymouth (Cont'd)

10 Plymouth.

11 Plymouth Pottery Co., about 1850.

Shelton (New Hall) (1-34)

The New Hall Pottery was founded in 1777 by Hollins, Keeling, Turner, Warburton, Clowes, and Bagnall. The factory suspended operations in 1825 after making both pottery and porcelain. In 1842 the works were in the hands of Hackwood & Co. From 1856 to 1862, Cookson & Harding. From 1862 W. & J. Harding.

The firm of Ridgway was started by Job Ridgway in 1794. The Cauldon factory was built in 1802. John Ridgway & Co. from 1814. Then J. & W. Ridgway, W. Ridgway and W. Ridgway & Son in that order. In 1836 the name changed to W. Ridgway, Morley, Wear & Co. In 1859 Brown-Westhead, Moore & Co. were the successors. W. B. & F. T. Moore operated the firm from 1882. Later it was titled Cauldon, Ltd. The Royal Crown and the Royal Arms were frequently used in the marks after 1850.

1, 2 Early New Hall marks. Painted in red.

3 New Hall. Mark in black.

4 New Hall. Mark of later period.

5 New Hall. After 1810. On luster ware.

6 1842-1856. Hackwood & Co. Impressed.

7 1856-1862. Cookson & Harding. Impressed.

8 Samuel Hollins. Latter half 18th century.

9 T. Fletcher & Co. 1786-1810.

10, 11 R. & J. Baddeley (1780-1806), then J. & E. Baddeley.

12 Hicks & Meigh. 1806-1820. Hicks, Meigh, & Johnson. 1820-1836.

13-17 1794-1859. Ridgways.

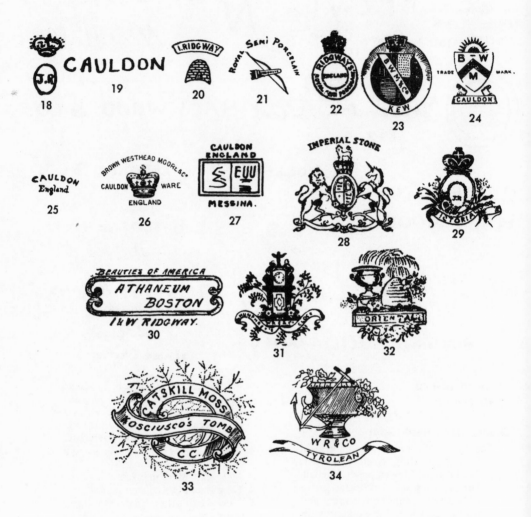

Shelton (Cont'd)
- **18, 19** After 1850. Ridgways.
- **20, 21** 1794-1859. Ridgways.
- **22** After 1850. Ridgways.
- **23, 24** After 1859. Brown-Westhead,

Moore & Co.
- **25-27** After 1891.
- **28** After 1850.
- **29-34** Various devices titling patterns. Ridgways.

SPODE SPODE

1   2   3   3a

 SPODE
Felspar Porcelain

4   5

  Spode's Imperial

6   7   8   9   10

SPODE, SON
& COPELAND   SPODE & COPELAND   COPELAND & GARRETT

11   12   13

C & G

14   15   16   17   18   19   20

Staffordshire

The potters and manufactories in this county are treated separately under the various towns and villages. The towns of Burslem, Cobridge, Etruria, Fenton, Hanley, Lane Delph, Lane End, Longton, Shelton, Stoke, and Tunstall are among those included under Staffordshire. In 1786 there were more than 80 different potters in this district, by 1802 there were more than 150.

Stoke-on-Trent (1-83)

Josiah Spode established in 1784 after potting from 1770. Josiah II was owner in 1797. Wm. Copeland was a partner but died in 1826. Josiah II died in 1827 and Josiah III in 1829. The name then changed from Spode, Son & Copeland to Copeland & Garrett, late Spode in 1833. After 1847 the firm became W. T. Copeland (Copeland, late Spode). In 1867 it was W. T. Copeland & Sons

Thomas Minton established a factory here in 1793, Herbert Minton and John Boyle operated it from 1836 to 1842. Hollins & Campbell were the proprietors before 1868. Colin Minton Campbell continued after that date. Porcelain was first made in 1800 and majolica in 1850.

Spode (1-37)

1-3 Early marks in red, blue, black, puce or gold. Sometimes impressed.

3A Impressed on early wares.

4, 5 Printed.

6, 7 Early 19th century. On Ironstone.

8-10 Early 19th century. Printed.

11, 12 Spode, Son & Copeland. Impressed or printed before 1833.

13, 14 Copeland & Garrett. 1833-1847. These marks generally accompanied by the name of the pattern.

15 After 1847.

16-20 Copeland & Garrett. 1833-1847.

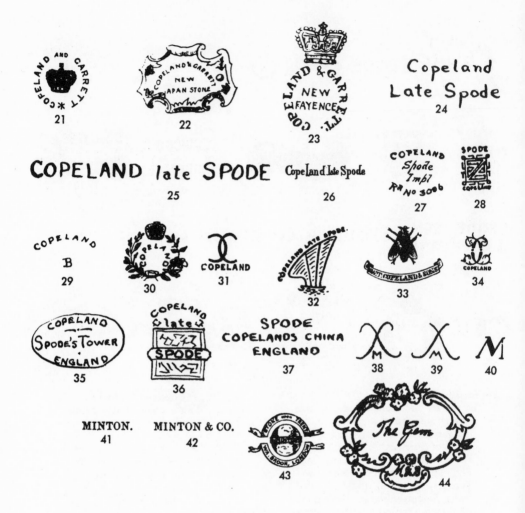

Stoke-on-Trent (Cont'd)
Spode—1-37
21-23 Copeland & Garret. 1833-1847.
24-26 W. T. Copeland. 1847-1867.
27-30 W. T. Copeland. 1847-1867.
31 1847-1856.
32, 33 W. T. Copeland & Sons. From 1867.
34 From about 1867 into the 20th century. This mark with the word

"England" was used after 1891. With "Made in England" it is a recent mark.
35 20th century mark. In blue.
36, 37 Late 19th or early 20th century.
Minton (38-61)
38-42 Early marks in color. The word "Minton" was not impressed in the ware until after 1861.
43 Late 19th or early 20th century.
44 Minton & Boyle. 1836-1842.

GREAT BRITAIN

Stoke-on-Trent (Cont'd)
Minton—38-61

45 Minton & Boyle. 1836-42. Mark impressed.
46 Minton & Co. Early mark.
47 In green after 1851.
48 From about 1868.
49 Late mark.
50 About 1870?
51 Late mark.
52 Earlier mark.
53 Late mark.
54 "B B"—Best Body. 1845-1861.
55 About 1823. Mark printed.

56 Colin Minton Campbell. After 1868.
57 Minton & Boyle. 1836 to about 1842.
58, 59 Louis Marc Solon, a decorator at Minton from 1870 to 1904.
60 Minton & Co. This mark impressed, raised or printed is a registration mark used by many English factories between 1842 and 1883. (See notice on Miscellaneous English Marks.)
61 Some Minton pieces were marked with these symbols to show the year of production.

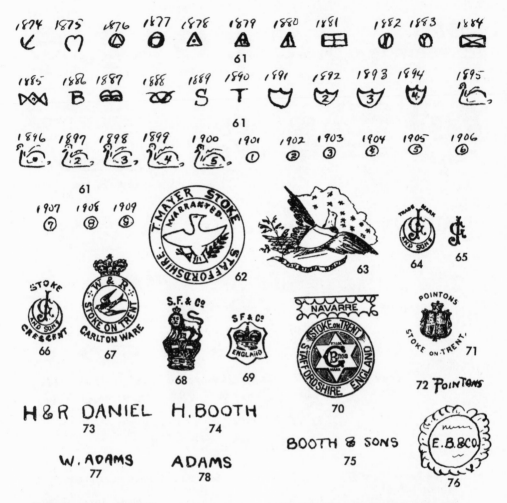

Stoke-on-Trent (Cont'd)

62, 63 T. Mayer. Circa 1829. Large trade with U. S.

64-66 G. Jones & Sons. Late 19th and early 20th century.

67 Wiltshaw & Robinson. Latter half 19th century.

68, 69 S. Fielding & Co. Latter half 19th century.

70 Grimwade Bros. This mark from 1891.

71, 72 Pointons. Late 19th century.

73 H. and R. Daniel. Established 1st quarter 19th century to 1845.

74 Hugh Booth. Up to 1789.

75 Booth & Sons. Here in 1802.

76 Ephraim Booth.

77 William Adams. Up to 1829. In addition to this there was a Wm. Adams at Tunstall (Greengates), Burslem, and Greenfield.

78 William Adams II. Succeeded his father in 1829.

GREAT BRITAIN

CLOSE & C<u>o</u>   BM

W. ADAMS & SONS
79

Late
W. ADAMS & SONS
STOKE-UPON-TRENT
80

81

W
82

WOLFE & HAMILTON
STOKE
83

PHILLIPS & CO.
1

Phillips & C<u>o</u>, Sunderland, 1813
2

J. PHILLIPS, HYLTON POTTERY
3

DIXON, AUSTIN, PHILLIPS & CO.
4

DIXON, PHILLIPS & CO.
5

W. DIXON
6

DIXON & CO.
7

DIXON & CO., SUNDERLAND POTTERY
8

DIXON, AUSTIN & CO.
9

DIXON & CO.
10

Wedgwood & Co., Ferrybridge
11

Tomlinson & Co.
12

Scott
13

Scott Brothers & Co.
14

Stockton
15

Wedgewood
16

W.S. & Co<u>s</u> Wedgewood
17

DAWSON
18

FORD
19

DAWSON & Co
5
20

Ford Pottery, South Hylton
21

THOMAS DAWSON & CO.
22

MALING
23

MOORE & CO.
STONEWARE
SOUTHWICK
24

Stoke-on-Trent (Cont'd)

79 W. Adams & Sons. About 1850.

80 Successors to the above. Close & Co.

81 Bernard Moore. Also the mark Moore Bros. with a crowned M. Comparatively modern pottery.

82 Thomas Wolfe. Established 1776. Mark impressed.

83 Wolfe & Hamilton. From 1790. Mark in red.

Sunderland District (1-26)

Numerous potteries here from early 18th century.

1, 2 Phillips & Co. From about 1800 to 1817.

3 J. Phillips. Established 1780.

4 From 1817. Dixon, Austin, Phillips & Co.

5 Successors to Dixon, Austin, Phillips & Co. Dixon, Phillips & Co.

6-10 Dixon & Co., Dixon, Austin & Co.; from about 1800.

11, 12 Tomlinson & Co. 1792-96; 1801-34.

13, 14 Scott Brothers & Co. 1788 to about 1837.

15, 16 Whalley, Smith & Skinner. From about 1800.

17 W. Smith & Co. From 1820. This mark illegalized in 1848.

18-21 Dawson & Co. (Ford Pottery). About 1800-1864. Marks impressed.

22 Thomas Dawson & Co. From about 1850.

23 Established 1762 and existed in the 20th century.

24 Moore & Co. Established 1789. This mark from 1803.

GREAT BRITAIN

WEDGWOOD & CO
25

ANTHONY SCOTT
& SONS
26

HAYNES, DILLWYN
& C°
CAMBRIAN POTTERY
SWANSEA
3

SWANSEA
5

Swansea
6

1

CAMBRIAN
POTTERY

SWANSEA

SWANSEA
⚔ 7

↑↑↑
8

SWANSEA

CAMBRIAN
2

G.H. & CO.
4

DILLWYN & CO.
9

OPAQUE CHINA
SWANSEA
10

DILLWYN
11

IMPROVED
STONE WARE
DILLWYN & Co.
12

BEVINGTON & CO,
SWANSEA
13

DILLWYN'S
ETRUSCAN
WARE
14

CUBA
DILLWYN & CO.
15

16
NANTGARW

Sunderland (Cont'd)

25 Tomlinson & Co. 1796-1800. (Ralph Wedgwood).

26 Anthony Scott & Sons. From about 1837.

Swansea, Wales (1-23)

Pottery factory established in 1764. George Haynes acquired the works in 1783 and renamed them the "Cambrian Pottery". In 1802 Lewis W. Dillwyn bought out his partner, Haynes. Porcelain was first made in 1814 about which time L. L. Dillwyn and Bevington were the proprietors. Dillwyn left in 1818. Bevington & Co. were owners until 1824 when the Dillwyns returned and operated the factory until 1850. The firm was Evans & Glasson until 1859 and then Evans & Co. until 1870

when the manufactory shut down. Swansea was not always marked. 17, 18 and 19 are marks of small firms in no way connected with the original Swansea factory.

1-4 Early marks. Before 1802. 1 about 1780.

5, 6 From 1814-1824. Generally red or impressed.

7, 8 These marks are a few years later than 5 and 6. In red or impressed.

9-11 From (1824-50).

12 On stoneware. Circa 1810-30.

13 Bevington & Co. 1817-1824.

14 About 1845-50.

15 (1802-1817) (1824-50).

16 This mark of the Nantgarw factory with or without the "CW" (China Works) was used 1814-1819 by William Billingsley, a decorator here from Nantgarw.

GREAT BRITAIN

CALLAND
SWANSEA
17

J.K.CALLAND & CO.
LANDORE POTTERY
18

Opaque China
B.B.&I.19

20

21

22

SWANSEA
23

TWIGG
1

Rockingham
2

ROCKINGHAM
3

MORTLOCK
4

5

ᴮᴿᴬᴹᴱᴸᴰ & CO'
6

BRAMELD ❋❋
7

8

GREEN
DON POTTERY
10

DON POTTERY
11

9 *Baguley*
Rockingham Works.

DON POTTERY
BARKER 12

Swansea (Cont'd)

17, 18 Established 1848 by John F. Calland. Closed 1856.

19, 20 Baker, Bevans & Irwin. 1813-1839.

21 Evans & Glasson. Successors to Dillwyn & Co. 1850-59.

22, 23 D. J. Evans & Co. 1859-1870.

Swinton (Rockingham) (1-16)

The Rockingham pottery factory was established at Swinton in 1757 by Edward Butler. Wm. Malpass was the proprietor from 1765 until 1778 when Thomas Bingley was the owner. Greens, Bingley & Co. was the combination that joined the Leeds factory to Rockingham from 1790 to 1800. John and William Brameld were the owners in 1806. Thomas, G. G., and J. W. Brameld introduced

porcelain in 1820. The factory closed in 1842. The Don Pottery was founded at Swinton in 1790 by John Green of the Leeds firm. The name was Green, Clarke & Co. in 1807. The works were bought in 1834 by Samuel Barker.

1 Twigg. Pottery about 1750.

2, 3 Rockingham. This mark generally accompanied by the word "Brameld".

4 Mortlock & Co. of London sold much of the Rockingham wares and impressed their name.

5-7 From 1806. Rockingham.

8, 9 These Rockingham marks usually printed in red were used from 1826 to 1842. From 1830 the prefix "Royal" was often used by this manufactory.

10, 11 Don Pottery. 1790-1834.

12 Don. 1834-1850.

73

Swinton (Cont'd)

13 Don. 1851-1882. Samuel Barker & Sons.

14 Don. After 1834. Printed.

15 Don. 1851-1882. Printed.

16 Don. 1851 to about 1855. Printed.

Tunstall (1-27)

1 James Beech. Before 1845.

2-4 Alfred Meakin. Established 1881.

5 Pitcairns, Ltd. This mark after 1891.

6 Boulton, Machin, & Tennant. Latter half 19th century.

7 Smith & Binnall.

8 Smith & Binnall?

9-10 T. G. and F. Booth. Latter half 19th century. (Tunstall?)

11 Bourne, Nixon & Co. About 1830.

12 Enoch Booth. Established 1750.

13 A. & E. Keeling. 1st quarter 19th century.

14 G. F. Bowers. 1st half 19th century.

15 Child. Established 1763. Mark stamped.

ADAMS 16

B.ADAMS 17

G F B RUBELLA 18

Heath 19

Adams & Co. 20

ADAMS & Co. 21

W. ADAMS & Co. 22

ADAMS TUNSTALL 23

ADAMS ENGLAND 24

25

ADAMS ENGLAND
26

27

1

2

3

WEDGWOOD & BENTLEY 4

W. & B. 5

WEDGWOOD & BENTLEY 6

WEDGWOOD 7

WEDGWOOD 8

WEDGWOOD 9

** WEDGWOOD 10

Wedgwood 11

Tunstall (Cont'd)

16 William Adams at Greengates. 1745-1805. There were potters at Burslem, Stoke and Greenfield with this same name. The modern firm of William Adams & Co. is working at Tunstall.

17 Benjamin Adams. 1805-1820.

18 G. F. Bowers. See 14.

19 Joseph Heath & Co. About 1825.

20 Probably used before 1790. Impressed. Adams.

21 On Jasper ware. Before 1790. Impressed. Adams.

22 Early Adams mark impressed.

23 19th century Adams mark impressed.

24, 25 Late 19th century. Printed.

26 After 1891. Printed.

27 After 1891. Printed.

Wedgwood (Etruria) (1-21)

The Wedgwood family was working at Burslem in the 17th century. Josiah was the first to gain fame, having started potting in 1739. Established at Burslem in 1759. Introduced Cream Ware in 1761. Produced black basaltes from 1766. Two years later he went into partnership with Thomas Bentley. Invented Jasper ware in 1775. It is doubtful if Josiah I made any other than experimental pieces of Jasper during his partnership with Bentley. Josiah II produced much of this ware. Bentley died in 1780. John, Josiah II and Thomas were Wedgwood's partners in 1790. He died in 1795. There were at least seven, if not twice that many, Wedgwoods working at the same time as Josiah I. Many used the mark "Wedgwood" for their wares. (See notice under Sunderland). The Etruria works were opened about 1770. It is doubtful if many pieces were marked between 1759 and 1769. Porcelain was made from 1812 and to 1816 and from 1878. The Wedgwood factory still operates today under the name Josiah Wedgwood & Sons, Ltd.

1-6 Wedgwood & Bentley. 1769-1780.

7-11 These marks impressed were used from before Bentley's partnership until the latter half of the 19th century. See 16.

GREAT BRITAIN

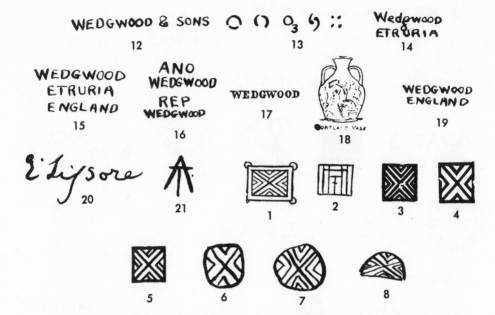

WEDGWOOD & SONS
12

O () O₃ ᘒ ::
13

Wedgwood
ETRURIA
14

WEDGWOOD
ETRURIA
ENGLAND
15

ANO
WEDGWOOD
REP
WEDGWOOD
16

WEDGWOOD
17

PORTLAND VASE
18

WEDGWOOD
ENGLAND
19

E Lysore
20

A
21

1   2   3   4

5   6   7   8

Wedgwood (Cont'd)

11 (See preceding page).

12 This mark may have been used from 1790 for a few years.

13 Various symbols used with the regular mark on earlier specimens.

14 From about 1840.

15 From about 1891.

16 "WEDGWOOD" with three accompanying letters was used from 1846. The "O" in the first mark represents the year 1860; "P", 1861, etc.

17 This mark used on porcelain from 1812 to 1816 in red, blue or gold.

18 On porcelain from 1878. Printed in black and other colors.

19 From 1891.

20 Emile Lessore. A painter. 1859-75.

21 Thomas Allen. A painter. 1875-1905.

Worcester (1-66)

Established 1751—by Dr. John Wall and Company. William Davis managed the factory until his death in 1783. Dr. Wall died in 1776. John and Joseph Flight were the operators in 1783 after the purchase of the factory by their father, Thomas. Martin Barr was a partner in 1792. Another Barr joined in 1807. George Barr went in in 1813 after the death of his father, Martin.

Robert Chamberlain & Son started business in 1786 by decorating Caughley wares. Flight, Barr & Barr and Chamberlain amalgamated in 1840. The original factory ceased operations in 1847 and Chamberlain continued with John and Frederick Lilly. In 1850 the owners were Chamberlain, Lilly, & Kerr. From 1852 to 1862 the name was Kerr & Binns. The Royal Worcester Porcelain Co. was formed in 1862. G. Solon succeeded W. H. Kerr in 1897 as manager.

The Grainger factory at Worcester existed from 1800 to 1846. James Hadley & Sons established in 1896 fused with the Royal Worcester factory in 1903. Edward Locke founded his works in 1895.

1-16 Various marks of the earliest period of the Worcester factory. The crescent mark also appears on Caughley. 1-8 usually in under-glaze blue.

GREAT BRITAIN

Worcester (Cont'd)

9-16 (See preceding page) 9-12 printed in colors and under glaze blue.

17 These are workmen's marks generally employed in conjunction with 1-12.

18-21 Before 1783. Imitation of the Meissen mark.

22 Before 1783. Imitation of the Sèvres mark.

23 Before 1783. Imitation of the Chantilly mark.

24-30 Before 1783.

31 About 1758.

32-33 Richard Holdship. About 1758.

34 Early mark.

GREAT BRITAIN

Worcester (Cont'd)

35, 36 Early marks.

37 Anchor in red. Similar to Chelsea mark. Early.

38 From 1783 to 1792. Flight. Impressed.

39 From 1783 to 1792. Flight. Blue under-glaze.

40, 41 From 1783 to 1792. Flight.

42, 43 1792-1807. Flight & Barr. Incised.

44, 45 1792-1807. Flight & Barr.

46, 47 Barr, Flight, & Barr. 1807-1813.

48, 49 Flight, Barr & Barr. 1813-1840.

50-55 Robert Chamberlain & Son. Established 1786. Later Walter Chamberlain. Merged with Flight, Barr & Barr in 1840.

56, 57 Kerr & Binns. 1852-1862.

58 1862-1891. Royal Worcester Porcelain Co. This same mark with the words "England" and "Made in England" is later.

GREAT BRITAIN

59

60

61

George Grainger
Royal China Works
Worcester

62

GRAINGER LEE & CO.
WORCESTER

63

64

65

66

THOMAS TOFT

1

RALPH TOFT 1677

2

I.L. 1638

3

G.R. 1651

4

I.W 1656

5

H.I. 1669

6

N.H 1678

7

I.E. 1697

8

IE:WS:1699:
WROTHAM

9

H.I. 1657

10

Absolon yarm

1

W.ABSOLON, YARM.

2

3

TERRA COTTA.
TRADE MARK

1

2

Worcester (Cont'd)

59 From 1891. Royal Worcester Porcelain Co.

60, 61 James Hadley & Sons. 1896-1903.

62 Grainger works established 1801 by Thomas Grainger. Grainger & Wood to 1812. Grainger, Lee & Co. from 1812.

63-65 Grainger & Co. 19th century marks. Printed. 64, 65—late marks.

66 Edward Locke & Co. From 1895.

Wrotham (1-10)

Many potters here in 17th century making slip ware. The wares were generally marked with initials and dates. The word Wrotham appears on some

pieces. A specimen dated 1739 is one of the latest known.

1-10 Initials of various potters. 10—Jull.

Yarmouth (1-3)

A manufactory was established here late in the 18th century by W. Absolon. Most of the wares were purchased elsewhere and decorated here.

1, 2 W. Absolon. From latter part 18th century.

3 W. Absolon. Impressed.

Miscellaneous English Marks (1-36)

1 Modern mark Tooth & Co. Burton-on-Trent.

2 S. & E. Collier. Reading. Modern mark.

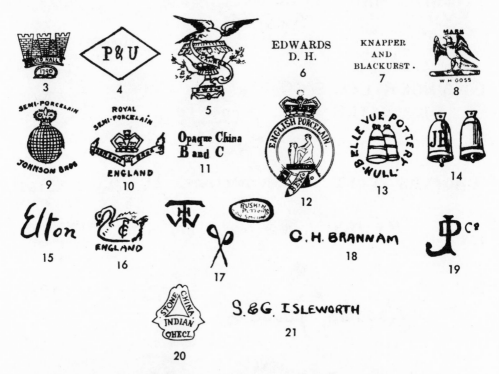

Miscellaneous English Marks (Cont'd)

3 Old Hall. Modern mark.

4 Poole & Unwin. Longton.

5 Podmore, Walker, & Co. 19th century mark.

6 James Edwards. From 1842. Fenton.

7 Knapper & Blackhurst. Successors to 6. Fenton.

8 W. H. Goss. Stoke-on-Trent. Late 19th century mark.

9, 10 Johnson Bros. Est. 1883.

11 Bridgwood & Clark. From 1857.

12 Bates, Elliott & Co. From 1790.

13, 14 Bellevue Pottery at Hull. 1802-1841. Est. by J. & J. Smith and Job Ridgway.

15 Sunflower Pottery, Clevedon, Som. Modern mark.

16 Charles Ford, Burslem.

17 W. Howson Taylor. Ruskin Pottery, Birmingham. Modern mark.

18 Brannam. Devon. Modern mark.

19 J. Dimmock & Co. Hanley. Modern mark.

20 Old Hall Porcelain Works. Hanley. Modern mark.

21 Isleworth. Est. 1760 by J. Shore & R. W. Goulding. Works moved to Hounslow in 1825 and to Wales in 1827.

GREAT BRITAIN

TRADE MARK

WEGGWOOD & Co.

22

THOMAS SHARPE
23

T. SHARPE
24

J. WALLEY'S Ware
25

EDGE & GROCOTT
26

MACINTYRE
27

R.W. MARTIN & BROS.
28

DUCROZ & MILLIDGE
29

REGINA
H&G
30

BOTT & CO
31

BELPER POTTERY
DENBY
32

BOURNE'S
POTTERIES
33

W. BURTON
CODNOR PARK
34

BOURNE'S POTTERIES
DENBY & CODNOR PARK
DERBYSHIRE
35

J. BOURNE & SON
36

Miscellaneous English Marks (Cont'd)

22 This is *not* a mark of the Josiah Wedgwood manufactory. Ralph Wedgwood—Burslem?

23, 24 Swadlincote. 1821-1838. Thomas Sharpe.

25 J. Walley at Cobridge in 1795. In 1835 the factory was Jones & Walley.

26 Edge & Grocott. About 1800-1830. Mark impressed.

27 1852-68. MacIntyre.

28 R. W. Martin & Bros. Incised on stoneware about 1900.

29 Ducroz & Millidge. About 1850. Lane End.

30 From 1853. Holland & Green. Longton.

31 Bott & Co. Early 19th century.

32 Belper Pottery established 1809 by Jager. This mark up to 1834.

33 1812-1834. Belper & Denby Potteries.

34 W. Burton. 1821-33.

35 1833-1861.

36 From mid 19th century into 20th century.

GREAT BRITAIN

A

B

A June 14, 1852 (Period—1842-1867).
B June 14, 1875 (Period—1868-1883).
From 1842 to 1883 an English registration mark showing the approximate date of manufacture was placed on four types of articles. Earthenware was one of them. The marks (A & B) in the margin are illustrative. Between 1842 and 1867 the letter at the top directly under the circle indicates the year of manufacture. The number at the right shows the day of the month. The letter at the left indicates the month of manufacture and the number at the bottom is a key to the manufacturer. The Roman numeral in the circle at top was used as follows: I for metal objects; II for wood; III for glass; and IV for earthenware. The approximate year of manufacture is indicated by the following letters:

X—1842	P—1851	Z—1860
H—1843	D—1852	R—1861
C—1844	Y—1853	O—1862
A—1845	J—1854	G—1863
I—1846	E—1855	N—1864
F—1847	L—1856	W—1865
U—1848	K—1857	Q—1866
S—1849	B—1858	T—1867
V—1850	M—1859	

The month is shown as follows:

C—January	I—July
G—February	R—August
W—March	D—September
H—April	B—October
E—May	K—November
M—June	A—December

Miscellaneous English Marks (Cont'd)
From 1868 to 1883 the numbers and letters were placed differently. The figure showing the day of the month was placed under the circle at top. The letter indicating the month is found at the bottom, the letter indicating the year of manufacture is found at the right and the manufacturer's parcel number is found at the left. In this second period the letters indicating the year are as follows:

X—1868	U—1874	Y—1879
H—1869	S—1875	J—1880
C—1870	V—1876	E—1881
A—1871	P—1877	L—1882
I—1872	D—1878	K—1883
F—1873		

The table of letters for the months is the same for both periods.

1. (Above) Jug. Pottery. English (Liverpool) late 18th Century. *Courtesy, Brooklyn Museum.*

2. (Right) Toddy Jug. Chinese Lowestoft XVIII Century (Late). Decorated with the arms of the U.S.A. *Courtesy, Metropolitan Museum of Art.*

3. Porcelain Group. Danish. Youth and Sleeping Shepherdess. About 1783. Copenhagen
Courtesy, Metropolitan Museum of Art.

4. Dish. Worcester Porcelain with scene from Aesop's Fables. English XVIII Century. *Courtesy, Metropolitan Museum of Art.*

5. Teapot. Porcelain. English Worcester. About 1770-1775. *Courtesy, Metropolitan Museum of Art.*

6. Plate. Chelsea "Lacework" dating from the 1770's. *Courtesy, Metropolitan Museum of Art.*

7. Plate. English, Staffordshire 19th Century. Clews "Dr. Syntax and the Bees." *Courtesy, Metropolitan Museum of Art.*

8. Figure. Merchant. German Porcelain. Frankenthal, about 1760. *Courtesy, Metropolitan Museum of Art.*

9. Ornament of Birds. Porcelain. English Chelsea. Late XVIII Century. *Courtesy, Metropolitan Museum of Art.*

10. Pair of Candlesticks. Chelsea. Showing a shepherd teaching a pretty shepherdess how to play a pipe. Dating 1765-1770 and illustrating the "bocage" or background of leaves. *Courtesy, Metropolitan Museum of Art.*

11. Chinese export porcelain with the arms of the State of New York. Late XVIII Century. *Courtesy, Metropolitan Museum of Art.*

12. Plates, Chelsea and Chelsea-Derby, showing a few of the many types of decorations used. *Courtesy, Metropolitan Museum of Art.*

13. Figure of man. Type known as "Ramlagh Figure". English, Derby XVIII Century (1765). *Courtesy, Metropolitan Museum of Art.*

14. Figure of Benjamin Franklin. English, Staffordshire by Enoch Wood. (1759-1840). *Courtesy, Metropolitan Museum of Art.*

15. Teapot. Decorated in Chinese style. English, Worcester about 1770. *Courtesy, Metropolitan Museum of Art.*

16. Soup Tureen, Salt Glaze. English, XVIII Century. *Courtesy, Metropolitan Museum of Art.*

17. Breakfast Set. Sevres porcelain. Second half of XVIII Century. *Courtesy, Metropolitan Museum of Art.*

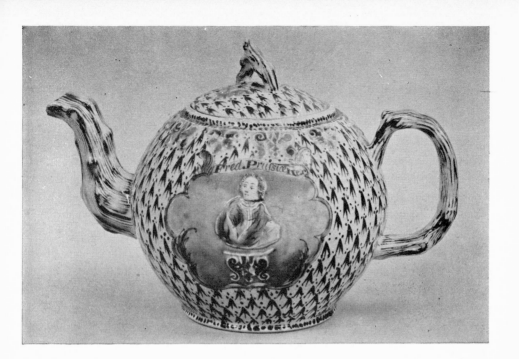

18. (Top) Teapot. Salt-Glaze. With portrait of the King of Prussia. Staffordshire, about 1705. 19. (Bottom) Vases, Royal Sevres porcelain, 1782 and 1789. Paintings with the medallions are by Dodin. *Courtesy, Metropolitan Museum of Art.*

20. Group, Chinese on Horseback. German porcelain modeled by F. A. Bustelli, Nymphenburg, about 1757-1762. *Courtesy, Metropolitan Museum of Art.*

22. The Duke of Cumberland represented as a Roman Emperor by Ralph Wood, about 1770-1780. *Courtesy, Metropolitan Museum of Art.*

21. Pitcher, porcelain, American, made by William Ellis Tucker, Philadelphia, Pa. 1828-1838. *Courtesy, Brooklyn Museum.*

23. (Top) Sweet meat dish. White Earthenware, 1771-1772 by Bonnin and Morris, Philadelphia, Pa. Capital P. in underglazed Blue. *Courtesy, Brooklyn Museum.* 24. (Bottom) Meissen, mid-eighteenth Century with characteristic decoration. *Courtesy, Metropolitan Museum of Art.*

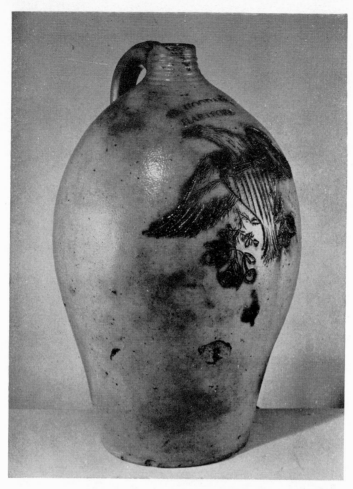

25. Jug, Stoneware, American, 1818-1838. Made by Daniel
Goodale, Hartford, Conn. *Courtesy, Brooklyn Museum.*

26. Vase Cups with medallions of cupids. English Chelsea Porcelain, c. 1765.
Courtesy, Metropolitan Museum of Art.

27. Teapot, white salt glazed stoneware. Designed by Daniel Greatbach and made by American Pottery Co., 1840-1850, Jersey City, N. J. *Courtesy, Brooklyn Museum.*

28. Lion, Flint enamel Earthenware with Cole Slaw decoration. American, about 1852-1858, designed by Daniel Greatback, made by Lyman Fenton & Company, Bennington, Vt. *Courtesy, Brooklyn Museum.*

30. Statuette groups. Soft paste porcelain, English Chelsea. William Pitt (1707-1778) receiving the gratitude of America (1765-1775). *Courtesy, Metropolitan Museum of Art.*

29. Pottery Figure, Eloquence. Maker, Enoch Wood, English (Burslem) about 1787. *Courtesy, Metropolitan Museum of Art.*

31. (Top) Pitcher, Rockingham glazed earthenware, rope design on handle, about 1845. Made at Salamander Works, Woodbridge, N. J. 32. (Bottom) Pitcher, Porcelain, about 1830. Made by Smith, Fife & Co., Philadelphia, Pa. *Courtesy, Brooklyn Museum.*

33. Majolica Dishes, Italian, 16th Century. Left to right: Sunburst pattern, Gubbio ware; Galatea and Polyphemus, Urbino ware; Peacock-eye pattern, Deruta ware. *Courtesy, Springfield (Mass.) Museum of Fine Arts.*

34. Three pieces of Bennington ware. American 19th Century. *Courtesy of Springfield (Mass.) Museum of Fine Arts.*

36. Figures of mountain miners, hard paste porcelain. German, Meissen, Kandler 1740-1750. Courtesy, Philadelphia Museum of Art.

35. Three color T'z'u Chou Ware. Chinese, Late Sung Dynasty, 960-1280 A.D. Courtesy, Springfield (Mass.) Museum of Fine Arts.

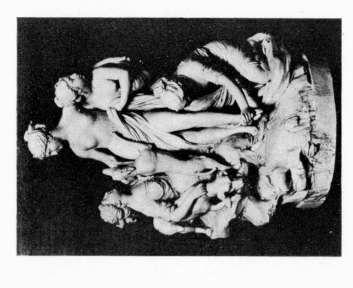

37. Group Biscuit, French Sevres, Louis Simon Boizot (1743-1809). Scratched on side of base, "4" and "LR." Scratched in clay on the under side of base before firing is the outline of the Bastille and "prise de la bastille le 14 Juillet 1789." 38. (Right) Another group, same maker, same markings on side of base. Scratched in clay on under side of base before firing, "Juillet" and below it, possibly "17(9)1." *Courtesy, Philadelphia Museum of Art.*

39. Tin-enameled Majolica, lustred Italian, Deruta, about 1530. Head of Holofernes, Pirota mark on back. *Courtesy, Philadelphia Museum of Art.*

40. Majolica plate, Italian, by Francesco Xanto Avelli de Rovigo. Urbino, lustred at Gubbio, dated 1531. *Courtesy, Philadelphia Museum of Art.*

41. Sugar Bowl. Tin-enameled, soft-paste porcelain. Chantilly, 1726-1735. Horn in red. *Courtesy, Philadelphia Museum of Art.*

42. Sauce-boot and Mug. Soft-paste porcelain. English, Lowestoft, 1780 and 1800. Figure "8" in blue on base of mug. *Courtesy, Philadelphia Museum of Art.*

43. Pot-pourri vase. Soft-paste porcelain. French, Sevres, 1757. Double cipher with date and letter "E" below, in blue. *Courtesy, Philadelphia Museum of Art.*

44. Vase. Soft-paste porcelain. English, Chelsea, about 1760. *Courtesy, Philadelphia Museum of Art.*

1

2

3 *Dublin*

Be*lfast* 1724 M
H•R
1724
4

DONOVAN
5

Ireland (1-5)

Works were founded at Belleek in 1857. In Dublin John Chambers was working from 1739 to 1751 when Crisp & Co. were his successors. Capt. Delamain established works here about 1755. The firm was Wilkinson & Delamain in 1769. Ackers & Shelly had a pottery in this place about 1770.

In Belfast Greg. Stephenson & Ashmore were in operation in 1792. Victor Coats had a pottery here in 1793.

In Wexford, Thomas Claugher (1790), Thomas Hardin (1767), and William Robb & Co. (1803) had factories.

In Limerick a Delft factory was founded by Stritch & Bridson from 1762 to 1770. John Hawkes & Co. were here about 1818.

1, 2 Belleek. From 1857. Mark in color or stamped. There is a modern firm here.

3 Earthenware factory in Dublin est. about 1755.

4 On Delft.

5 A decorator at the factory indicated by 3. He also worked for Spode and Minton. About 1800. Donovan.

Scotland (1-13)

Among numerous manufactories here whose marks are not shown are: Young Bros. from 1862; Ferguson, Miller & Co.; Grangemouth; North British Pottery in 1878; A. Balfour & Co. in 1900; The Saracen Pottery founded in 1875; Port Dundas Pottery from 1819; the Hyde Park Potteries of McAdam from 1837; Henry Kennedy's Barrowfield Pottery est. in 1866, now Henry Kennedy & Sons; A. W. Buchan & Co.; the Fife Pottery of R. Heron & Son here in 1900; and the Alloa Pottery from late 18th century, owned in 1900 by W. & J. Bailey.

GREAT BRITAIN

Scotland (Cont'd)

1 Fowler, Thompson & Co. 1st quarter 19th century. Prestonpans.
2 R. Cochran & Co. From 1855. Glasgow.
3, 4 Cochran & Fleming. Successors to 2. Glasgow. The trade mark is a seated figure with a trident in her hand.
5 Clyde Pottery Co. At Greenock in 1900.

6 Grosvenor & Son. Established 1869.
7 W. A. Gray. Est. 1857 in Portobello.
8 D. Methven & Sons. Working in 1878.
9 Garnkirk Co. From about 1870.
10 Scott Brothers at Portobello from late 18th century.
11-13 J. & M. P. Bell & Co. From 1842.

FOWLER , THOMPSON & Co.

1

R. COCHRAN & CO. GLASGOW

2

COCHRAN & FLEMING GLASGOW 3

C & F

4

C. P. CO.

5

GROSVENOR & SON

6

W. H. GRAY & SONS

7

D. METHVEN & SONS

8

GARNKIRK

9

SCOTT PB

10

J & M P. B & Cᵒ

11

12

13

HOLLAND

Porcelain factory established at Weesp in 1764, closed in 1771. Transferred to Oude Loosdrecht in 1772. Removed to Oude Amstel in 1784 and closed again near end of 18th century. George Dommer & Co. established a factory there at this time, but it ceased operation in 1810. A. La Fond & Co. started work in Amsterdam at that time. About 1775 a porcelain manufactory opened at The Hague and closed 10 years later. At Arnheim there was a fayence factory from 1780 to about 1785.

HOLLAND

Holland (Cont'd)

1-4 Weesp. 1764-1771. Porcelain. 1, 2—In blue and red. 3, 4—In blue.

5-7 Oude Loosdrecht. 1772-84. Blue, red, or incised.

8-10 Oude Amstel. 1784-c. 1800. George Dommer & Co. used mark 8 until 1810. 9—A. Dareuber. In blue.

11 Amsterdam. Mark traced in blue.

12 A. La Fond & Co. Amsterdam. 1st quarter 19th century.

13 The Hague. c. 1775-85. The mark of the stork in blue is found in various forms. Some Tournai porcelain was decorated here. The stork in underglaze blue appears on Hague porcelain, and in overglaze blue on Tournai decorated at Hague.

14-16 Weesp. 1764-71.

17 1671-1708. On red ware.

18, 19 Arnheim. Fayence. About 1780.

H. Van Laun. 19—Amstel?

20 On late 17th century red ware.

21 The Hague. 18th century mark in red.

Holland, Delft

Many factories here in 17th century. In 1808 only these of the earlier ones remained; The Ewer; The Flowerpot; The Claw; The Porcelain Bottle; The Greek "A"; The Three Bells; and The Rose. In 1850 only the Three Bells existed. The Porcelain Bottle was revived in 1876 by Thooft & Labouchere. The majority of Delft marks are potters' signatures and initials.

1 The Axe (De Dessel). About 1696.

2 The Boat (De Boot). Est. 1661. 2—From 1675.

Holland, Delft (Cont'd)

3, 4 The Boat (De Boot). Est. 1661.
3—From 1707. 4—From 1759.

5-10 The Claw (De Klauw). Est.
1662. 5 from 1662. 6 from 1702.
7—1750. 8, 9 from 1764. 10—1830-
1850, J. van Putten & Co.

11-16 The Double Jug (De Dubbelde
Schenk Kan). Est. 1648. 11 from
1648. 12—1675. 13—1689. 14—
1714. 15—1721. 16—1764.

17-19 The Fortune (De Fortuyn).
Est. 1691. 17—from 1691. 18—1706.
19—1759.

20-22 The Gilded Flower Pot (De
Vergulde Bloompot). Est. 1693. 20
from 1693. 21—1761. 22—1761.

23-27 The Greek "A" (De Griekse
A). Est. 1645. 23 from 1645. 24—
1674. 25—1703. 26—1759. 27—
1765.

28 The Four Roman Heroes (De Vier
Helden van Rome). Est. 1713. 28
from 1713.

29-30 The Jug. (De Lampet Kan).
Est. 1759. 29 from 1759. 30—1780.

Holland, Delft (Cont'd)

31-34 The Metal Pot (De Metale Pot). Est. 1639. 31 from 1639. 32—1667. 33—1691. 34—1738.

35-36 The New Moor's Head. (De Jonge Moriaan's Hooft). Est. 1720. 35—from 1720. 36—Mark of widow of founder.

37-41 The Old Moor's Head (De Oude Moriaans Hooft). Est. 1648. 37 from 1648. 38—1661. 39—1680. 40—1759. 41—1764.

42-44 The Peacock (De Paauw). Est. 1651. 42 from 1651. 43—1701. 44—

1732. Works closed in 1790.

45, 46 The Porcelain Axe. (De Porseleine Byl). Est. 1679. 45 from 1679. 46—1759.

47-52 The Porcelain Bottle (De Porseleine Fles). Est. 1660. 47 from 1660. 48—1698. 49—1759. 50—1770. 51—1795. 52 from about 1890.

53-55 The Porcelain Dish (De Porseleine Schotel). Est. 1701. 53—1759. 54—1764. 55—1764.

56-59 The Roman (De Romeyn). Est. 1671. 56 from 1671. 57—1697. 58—1759. 59—1764.

HOLLAND

Holland, Delft (Cont'd)

60-64 The Rose (De Roos). Est. 1675. 60 from 1675. 61—Two marks from 1675. 62—1732. 63—1759. 64—1803. van Putten & Co. from 1830.

65-69A The Stag (T'hart). Est. 1661. 65, 66—early marks. 67—1707. 68—1757. 69—1750-64. 69A—1750-64.

70-75 The Star (De Star). Est. 1690. 70 from 1690. 71—1705. 72—1720. 73 — 1720. 74—1759. 75 — Two marks from 1763.

76-78 The Three Bells (De Drie Klokken). Est. 1671. 76—factory mark. 77—1675. 78—1764. From 1830, Jan van Putten & Co.

79-81 The Three Cinder Tubs (De Drie Astonne). Est. 1672. 79—from 1672. 80—1759. 81—1720.

82-86 The Three Porcelain Bottles. (De Drie Porseleine Fleschen). Est. 1671. 82, 83 from 1671. 84—1690. 85—1701. 86—1764.

87 The Two Little Boats (De Twee Scheepjes). Est. 1756. 87 from 1756.

88, 89 The Two Savages (De Twee Wildemans). Est. 1750. 88 from 1750. 89—W. van Beek.

90 Rare mark on pieces similar to Chinese porcelain.

91 De Ster. 1720-1725.

ITALY

Pottery was made in Italy from the earliest times and many of the various pieces can be best classified under the broad term "Majolica". Specimens of this ware can be categorized under particular manufactories if information or knowledge of the various characteristics (color, design, paste, etc.) is known. If not, with few exceptions it is inadvisable to determine the origin of any piece by the mark alone.

Majolica can be described as earthenware coated with an enamel that is sometimes lustered.

Generally in early services only the largest pieces were marked.

Bologna

Fine imitations of old majolica.

1 Bologna—From 1849. Angel Minghetti.

Caffaggiolo

Noted for beautiful majolica 15th through 17th century. The words "Glovis", "Semper" (SPR) and the initials SPQF and SPQR are frequently found on this ware.

2-31 Caffaggiolo—15th, 16th and 17th century marks on Majolica.

Capo-di-Monte (32-41)

(1743-1759) (1771-1821) Established 1743 by Charles III near Naples. Charles vacated crown in 1759. In 1771 his successor Ferdinand IV revived the works at Portici. They were removed to Naples in 1773 where the Ginori factory at Doccia absorbed many of the old models in 1821. Soft paste porcelain was made from 1743 to 1759. From 1771 hard and soft paste and biscuit were made. Old Capo di Monte is rare, but the market today is flooded with spurious specimens generally marked in blue with a crowned "N". Late factories in France, Germany, and Italy produced these recent specimens. (See Doccia). Little is known of early marks.

32-34 1771-1773. Sometimes in red. Rex Ferdinandus.

35 From 1771. Also see notice above.

36 In gold. (Le Nove?)

37 In blue (Vinovo?)

38 After 1771. (Ginori?)

39 Buen Retiro?

40, 41 Incised, Modellers names.

Castel-Durante (42-47)

The work here was similar to that at Urbino. Many pieces were sent to Gubbio for lustred decoration.

42-47 Castel-Durante. 16th and 17th century marks.

Castelli (48-53)

Majolica factories here. G. Rocco, Capelletti, Fuina, Cianico and Rossetti are names associated with this place in 18th century.

48-53 Castelli. 16th and 17th century marks. 51-B. Gentile. 52, 53 C. Gentile.

Cornaro (54)

54 Cornaro.

Deruta (55-61)

Majolica made here from 16th century. Occasionally with lustre decoration.

55 Mark from 16th century.

ITALY

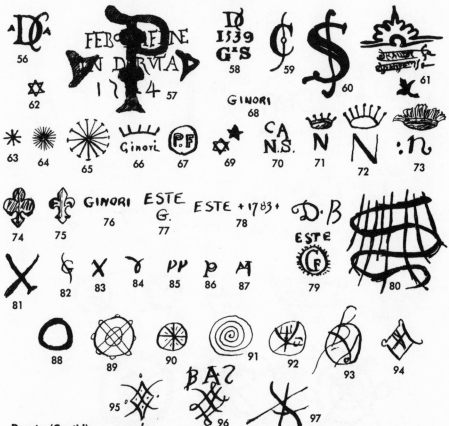

Deruta (Cont'd)
56-61 Marks from 16th century.

Doccia (Ginori) (62-76)
Established 1735 by Carlo Ginori. The work here in the 18th century was similar to that at Le Nove. In 1821 the Capo-di-Monte molds were secured and copies of old Capo-di-Monte were made, especially in the past 50 years. A good quality majolica was also produced. (See Capo-di-Monte).

62-70 18th century or early 19th century marks similar to Le Nove. 67 Fanciullacci. 68 Also on specimens after 1821.

71-76 After acquiring the Capo-di-Monte molds in 1821 the Marchese Ginori marked his pieces as shown. 72—Most modern pieces, some not 20 years old, are marked in this way generally in blue. 75, 76—Generally impressed.

Este, near Padua (77-79)
Fayence and porcelain made here from about 1750 well into the 19th century. J. Varion and G. Franchini about 1780.

77
78 Mark stamped.
79 Domenick Brunnello.

Fabriano (80)
Majolica from mid 15th century.
80 Fabriano. Early 16th century mark.

Faenza (81-140)
In the 16th century the great fayence center of Italy was at this place. In 1850 Farini established a majolica factory here.
81 Circa 1500.
82-86 15th century.
87 Faenza or Florence. 1460.
88
89-93 Casa Pirota factory. c. 1530.
94-97 Casa Pirota?

ITALY

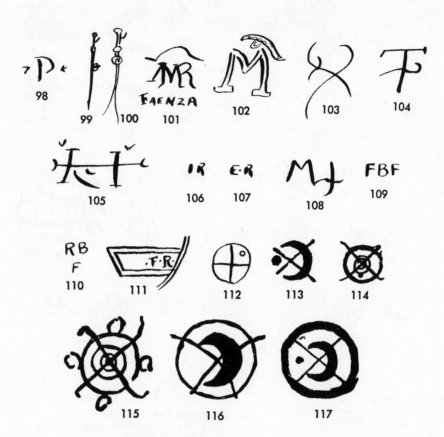

Faenza (Cont'd)
98 1533.
99, 100 c. 1550.
102 1527.
105 Atanasio factory?
106 1508.
107 1520-30.
108 1546.
109 Francisco Ballanti. 18th century.
110 Benini. 1777-8.
111-117 Casa Pirota. c. 1530.

118 Casa Pirota, 1508.
119 Casa Pirota.
120 Casa Pirota?
121 c. 1540.
122, 123 Atanasio?
124, 125 c. 1520.
126 Casa Pirota?
127 Baldasara Manera. 1534.
128 1575.
129 c. 1530. Baldasara Manera.
130-132

Faenza (Cont'd)

133 Vergiliotto. 17th century.

136 c. 1510.

137-140 Miscellaneous.

140A A. Farini. 1850-1878.

140B A. Farini. From 1878.

Florence (141-146)

One of the earliest European porcelain factories was here under the patronage of Francesco I di Medici about 1580. It is reputed that porcelain was made in Venice as early as 1470.

141 15th century.

142 Cantagalli. Late 19th century. Fayence.

143 On 18th century majolica.

144-146 On early European porcelain. Medici. About 1580.

Forli (1-5)

Majolica factories here from 14th century.

1-5 15th and 16th century marks on majolica. 2—Deruta? 3—1523. 5—1485-90.

Genoa (6-12)

Majolica made here as early as 1548.

6 17th century mark.

7 18th century mark.

ITALY

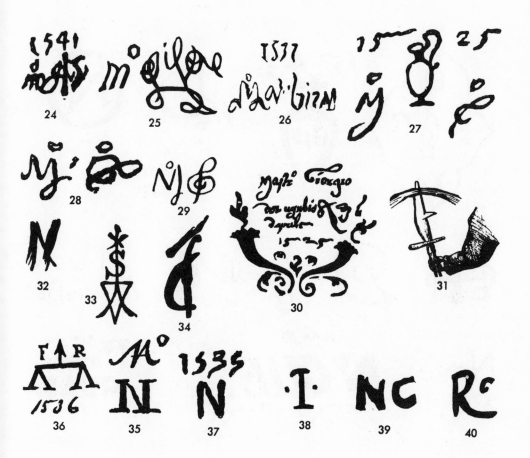

Gubbio (Cont'd)

13-30 Maestro Giorgio Andreoli, 1st half 16th century.
31-40 Miscellaneous early marks.

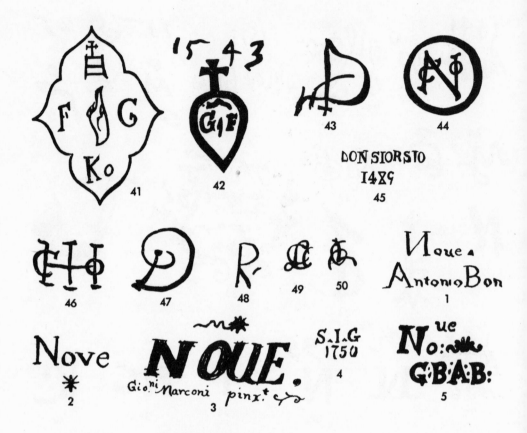

Gubbio (Cont'd)
  41-47 Miscellaneous early marks.
  48 Prestino. 1536-57.
  49-50 Carocci, Fabbri & Co. 19th century.
Le Nove, Bassano (1-16)
  G. B. Antonibon established a pottery here about 1760. Many other factories sprung up after that time. Soft paste porcelain was made until 1835.
  1-3 From about 1760.
  5 From about 1760. Giovanni Battista Antonibon.

ITALY

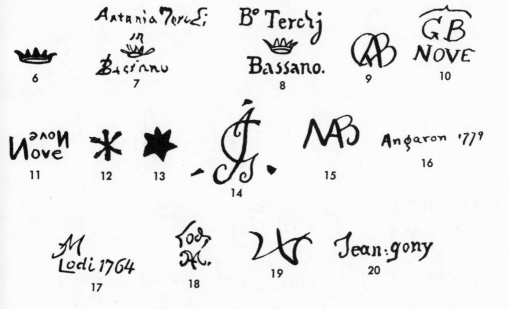

6-8 Antonio and Bartolomeo Terchi.
9 Early 18th century.
10 G. Baroni. Early 19th century.
12, 13 From 1760. Mark in red or
gold.
14, 15 Manardi. Late 17th century.
16 Mark incised.
Lodi (17-19)
Fayence made here in 17th and 18th
centuries.
17-19 17th century marks.
Maurienne (20)
20

ITALY

ITALY

Naples (Cont'd)
  15-17 Variations of 5.
Padua (18-23)
  Majolica made here from 16th century.
  20 1563.
  21 1564.
  22, 23 1555.
Pavia (24, 25)
  Majolica.
  25 About 1710.
Pesaro (1-9)
  Potteries here from 14th century.
  1 1723.
  2 Casali and Caligari.
  3 Early 16th century.
  4 1520-30.
  5 About 1510.
  6, 7

8 Terencio.
9 Magrini & Co. From 1870.
Pisa (10)
  Majolica.
  10 16th century mark.
Ravenna (11)
  Majolica.
  11 16th century mark.
Rimini (12, 13)
  A few majolica specimens known, all
    dated between 1535 and 1635.
  12-13 1538.
Rome (14-18)
  14-16 Late 16th and early 17th cen-
    tury marks.
  17 1769.
  18 1790-1831. G. Volpato. On bisque
    and white pottery.

ITALY

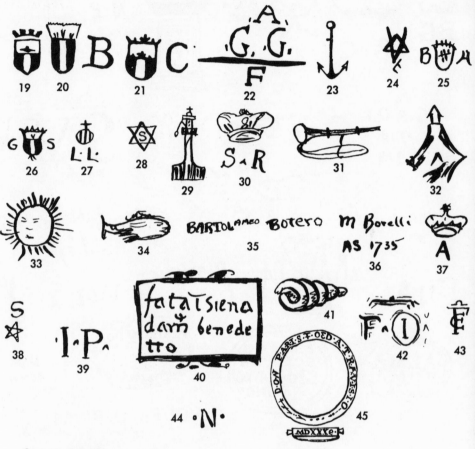

Savona (19-38)

A pottery was established at Albissola near Savona in the early 17th century. The marks shown are all 17th and 18th century.

19-23 17th century.
24 c. 1700. Siccardi.
25, 26 18th century.
27 About 1670. Luigi Levantino.
28 Siccardi?
29 Levantino (See Genoa).
30 S. Rubatto.
31 c. 1667. Chiodo.
32 Bartolomeo Guidobono.
33 G. Salomone.

34 Pescetto.
35 c. 1729.
36 M. Borelli. Late 18th century
37
38 Siccardi. c. 1700.

Siena (39-43)

An excellent factory which in its early years produced wall or floor tiles.

39, 40 About 1510-20.
41, 42
43 Ferdinando Campini?

Treviso (44-46)

Majolica.

44
45 1538.

ITALY

Treviso (Cont'd)

46 Fratelli Fontebasso. In gold. Late 18th century.

Turin (47-58)

Fayence made here in 16th and 17th centuries.

47-50

51 1577.

52 Rosetti.

53 c. 1629.

54-57

58 About 1820.

Urbino (59-89)

Various important potteries here from 16th century.

59 1535.

60

61, 62 Orazio Fontana. c. 1560.

63

64 Orazio Fontana.

65 Flaminio Fontana. c. 1583.

66

67 Nicola Pellipario. c. 1530.

68, 69 Orazio Fontana.

70 Nicola Pellipario.

71-73 c. 1540. F. Xanto Avelli.

74, 75

76 Nicola Pellipario. c. 1530.

ITALY

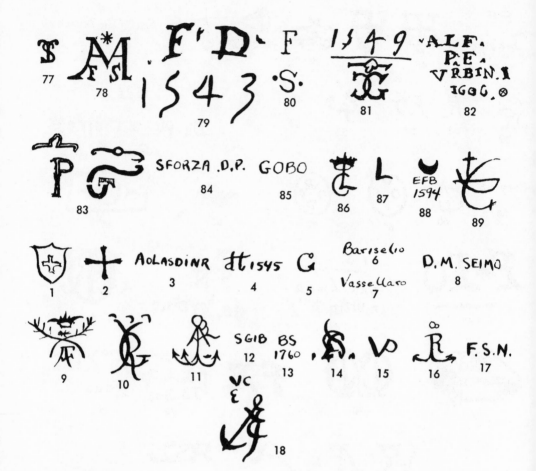

ITALY

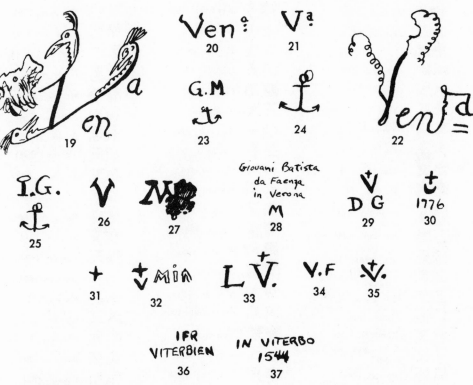

Venice (Cont'd)

19-22 Vezzi. 1719-1740. Marks generally painted in blue. Porcelain. Vezzi wares were unmarked until 1725.

23-25 Cozzi. 1764-1812. Marks generally painted in red. Porcelain.

26 Hewelke. 1758-1763. Mark incised. Porcelain. This mark is also attributed to the Vezzi factory.

Verona (27, 28)
Majolica.
27
28 1563.
Vinovo (29-35)
Majolica and porcelain factory established here in 1776 by G. V. Brodel.

V. A. Gioanetti was the proprietor in 1780. Factory closed in 1815.

29 Gioanetti. c. 1776. This mark found on both majolica and porcelain.

30 Mark painted in grey. Porcelain.

31 Mark painted in black. Porcelain.

32 Mark painted in grey and incised. Porcelain.

33-35 About 1780-1815. Porcelain.

Viterbo (36, 37)
Majolica, 16th century.
36 16th century.
37 16th century. This mark on a ribbon.

JAPAN

Ken-tok, 1370.	Yei-show, 1504.	Show-tok, 1711.
Bun-tin, 1372.	Dai-jei, 1521.	Kiyo-ho, 1717.
Ten-du, 1375.	Kiyo-rok, 1528.	Gen-bun, 1736.
Ko-wa, 1380.	Di-yei, 1532.	Kwan-po, 1741.
Gen-tin, 1380.	Ko-dsi, 1555.	Yen-kiyo, 1744.
Mei-tok, 1393.	Yei-rok, 1558.	Kwan-jen, 1748.
O-yei, 1394.	Gen-ki, 1570.	Ho-reki, 1751.
Show-tiyo, 1428.	Ten-show, 1573.	Mei-wa, 1764.
Yei-kiyo, 1429.	Bun-rok, 1592.	An-jei, 1772.
Ka-kitsu, 1441.	Kei-chiyo, 1596.	Ten-mei, 1781.
Bun-an, 1444.	Gen-wa, 1615.	Kwan-sei, 1789.
Ho-tok, 1449.	Kwan-jei, 1624.	Kiyo-wa, 1801.
Kiyo-tok, 1452.	Show-ho, 1644.	Bun-kwa, 1804.
Ko-show, 1455.	Kei-an, 1648.	Bun-sei, 1818.
Chiyo-rok, 1457.	Show-o, 1652.	Ten-po, 1834.
Kwan-show, 1460.	Mei-reki, 1655.	Ko-kua, 1844.
Bun-show, 1466.	Man-dsi, 1658.	Ka-yei, 1848.
O-nin, 1467.	Kwan-bun, 1661.	Bun-se, 1854.
Bun-mei, 1469.	Yen-po, 1673.	Man-yen, 1860.
Chiyo-kiyo, 1487.	Ten-wa, 1681.	Bun-kin, 1861.
En-tok, 1489.	Tei-kiyo, 1684.	Gen-di, 1861.
Mei-o, 1492.	Gen-rok, 1688.	Kei-o, 1865.
Bun-ki, 1501.	Ho-yei, 1704.	Mei-di, 1868.
1	**2**	**3**

4   **5**

The notice on this subject is necessarily short because of the limited interest in Japanese ceramics. Pottery was made in Japan from the earliest times. Porcelain was first produced about 1515. The marks on Japanese pottery are generally stamped, painted or incised. Stamps and seals are frequently found. Much old porcelain is unmarked and generally it was not until the 19th century that the individual potters put their names on their wares. Important oriental marks were frequently copied. Many Japanese marks are written in Chinese.

1-3 Japanese dates. (Nengo).

4 This mark with other characters belongs to the 19th century. Dai Nippon.

5 Dai Nippon Kutani zo. "Made at Kutani in Great Japan." This is illustrative of a great many 19th century marks.

LUXEMBOURG

Luxembourg (1-6)

A pottery factory was established here in 1767 by the Boch Brothers. In 1795 the owner was Pierre-Joseph Boch. Hard paste porcelain was made from 1806. The firm name in the 19th century was Villeroy & Boch (Mettlach). For additional marks see the Luxembourg and Mettlach notices under Germany.

1-6 Early marks. Luxembourg.

NORWAY

Norway (1, 2)

A fayence factory was operated at Herreboe by Peter Hofnagel from 1758 to 1770.

1, 2 1758-1770.

PERSIA, TURKEY, SYRIA
POLAND

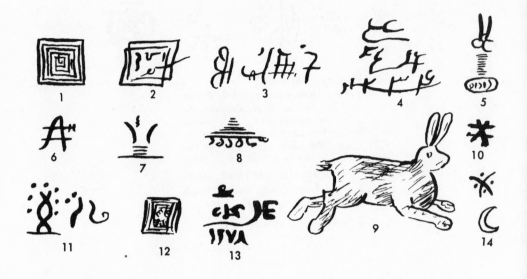

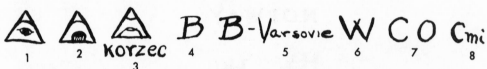

Poland (1-8)

Many potteries here from the 12th century. The Belvedere factory at Warsaw was established in 1774. M. Oginski founded pottery works at Telechany at the end of the 18th century and at Warsaw Wolff erected works in 1775. The Korzec porcelain factory was started in 1803 and abandoned a few years later. Information on the Proskau manufactory will be found under "Germany".

1-3 Korzec. Hard paste porcelain. From 1803.

4, 5 Belvedere. 1774 to about 1800. Mark over-glaze.

6 Wolff at Warsaw. From 1775.

7 M. Oginski at Telechany. Late 18th century.

8 Chmeloff.

Persia, Turkey and Syria (1-14)

Little porcelain was made in the Near East. The pottery is strong in color and floral decorations are common. Marks are found infrequently and those presented are merely representative of the style.

1 On blue and white fayence. 16th or 17th century.

2 17th century.

3 19th century.

4 Mohammed Ali. Early 19th century.

5-8 Blue and white fayence. 19th century.

9 Glazed pottery. 16th or 17th century.

10-13 Miscellaneous.

14 On Turkish porcelain.

PORTUGAL

Portugal (1-14)

With the exception of the Vista Alegre factory mostly fayence was made here.

1 Lisbon. About 1833.

2 Mafra at Caldas. About 1870. Copies of Palissy and Staffordshire ware.

3-5 Rato. 18th century marks on pottery in yellow and violet.

6 Lisbon.

7, 8 Vista Alegre. Established about 1790 and exists today. Hard paste porcelain.

9-10 Miragaia. About 1755.

11-13 Viana de Castello. 18th century.

14 Coimbra.

RUSSIA

Russia (1-32)

Many Russian pottery and porcelain manufactories are not shown here. Porcelain was first made at St. Petersburg about 1743. Little is known of the early marking.

St. Petersburg (1-21)

1-3 Early marks. After 1743. Porcelain.

4-6 Catherine II. 1762-96.

7 Emperor Paul. 1796-1801.

8 Alexander I. 1801-1825.

9 Nicholas I. 1825-1855.

10-11 Alexander II. 1855-1871.

12-15 Alexander II. 1871-1881. Starting with 1871, one dot was added to the mark yearly.

16, 17 Korniloff Brothers. From 1825.

18-21 Gardner. From 1758. At Moscow from about 1780. 18, 19 in blue.

Miscellaneous (22-32)

22 Mezer at Baranovka. From 1804. Porcelain. Mark stamped.

23-26 A. Popoff in Moscow. 1806-1872. Porcelain. Marks 25 and 26 are questionable

27 Kiev. M. Gulina. Porcelain.

28 Kiev.

29 Nicholas II. St. Petersburg. From 1894.

30 Mezer at Baranovka. From 1804. Porcelain.

31 S. T. Kuznetsoff. St. Petersburg.

32 Stawsk. 1843-47. Pottery.

SPAIN

Alcora (1-18)

A fayence and porcelain factory was established here about 1750. The "A" mark is believed to have been used from 1784.

1-5 From 1784. Porcelain. Mark in red, black, gold or incised.

6, 7 Painters marks. Alcora.

8 On fayence. Soliva was a painter.

9 On early fayence.

10, 11 Painter's marks.

12 Jose de Zaragoza.

13-18 Painter's marks.

Buen Retiro (19-50)

Sometimes called La China a soft paste porcelain manufactory was founded here in 1759 by Charles III. Hard paste was made after 1780. The factory closed in 1808. Fayence was also made. The fleur de lis mark is generally in blue. These wares are frequently confused with Capo di Monte.

19-44 1759-1808.

SPAIN

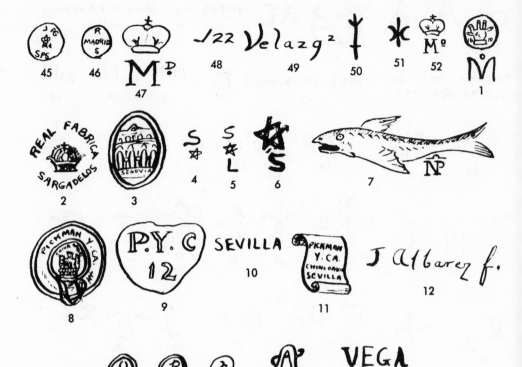

Buen Retiro (Cont'd)
45-50 1804-1808. 45, 46 and 47 are also attributed to Moncloa.

La Moncloa (51, 52)
Also known as Florida. Porcelain (hard and soft paste) and biscuit were made here from 1817 to 1849. These wares are frequently confused with Capo di Monte.
51, 52 1817-1849.

Manises (1)
Majolica made here from 15th century.
1 About 1610. Majolica.

Sargadelos (2)
2 19th century.

Segovia (3)
3 19th century.

Seville (4-7)
4-7 19th century marks.

Talavera (12)
Important fayence manufactory in 17th and 18th centuries.
12 17th or 18th century.

Valencia (13-16)
Noted for enamel tiles. Fayence from 15th century.
13-16 Valencia. 15th century marks on Hispano-Moresque wares.

Valladolid (17)
17

SWEDEN

Sweden (1-19)

A fayence manufactory was established at Rörstrand about 1725. Until 1760 the products were similar to Oriental and Delft ware. After that time the products were styled after the continental factories. A modern mark of Rörstrand is composed of the Royal Crown over the initials M. S. & Co.

At Marieberg a fayence and porcelain factory was founded in 1760 and prospered until about 1788

The fayence works at Stralsund were started in the early 18th century and continued until 1792.

1, 2 Rörstrand. About 1725-1758.
3 Rörstrand About 1780.
4-8 Rörstrand After 1758.
9 Marieberg. Dated Nov. 24, 1764. Ehrenreich, Director; Frantzen, painter.
10 Marieberg. About 1766-69. Berthevin, director.
11 Marieberg. Dated Oct. 14, 1768.
12-15 Marieberg. After 1769.
16-18 Stralsund. After 1766. "E" for Ehrenreich.
19 Gustafsberg. Fayence. 1820-1860.

SWITZERLAND

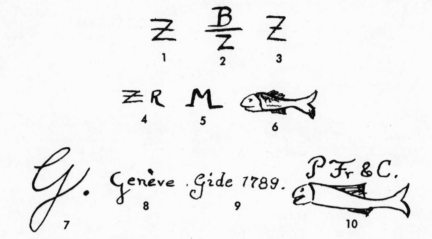

Switzerland (1-10)

Both pottery and porcelain were made at Zurich where a factory was established about 1763. Porcelain was manufactured until 1800. Porcelain works were established at Nyon about 1781 and closed about 1813. Wintherthur was noted for the manufacture of fayence stoves in the 17th and 18th century.

1-4 Zurich. From 1763. The mark is usually in blue.

5 Munster.

6-9 Nyon 1781-1813. Porcelain.

10 Nyon. Pfluger Bros. & Co.

UNITED STATES

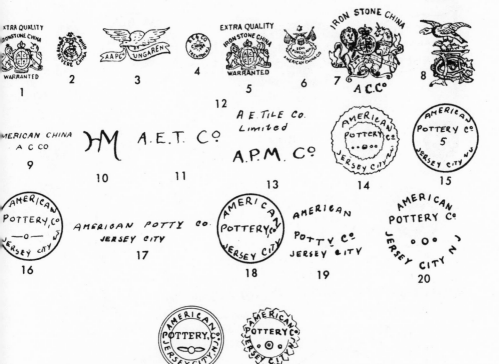

United States

1, 2 Akron China Co., Akron, O.

3 American Art Ceramic Co., Corona, N. Y. Established 1901.

4 American Art China Works, Trenton, N. J. Established 1891.

5, 6 American China Co., Toronto, Ohio. Established 1897.

7-9 American Crockery Co., Trenton, N. J. Established 1876.

10-12 American Encaustic Tiling Co., Zanesville, Ohio.

13 American Porcelain Mfg. Co., Gloucester, N. J. 1854-57. Impressed.

14-22 American Pottery Co., Jersey City, N. J. 1833-45. Impressed. Printed.

UNITED STATES

23, 24 American Pottery Mfg. Co.,
Jersey City, N. J. 1833-40. Marks
printed under-glaze.

25 American Terra-Cotta Co., Chicago,
Illinois.

26-35 Anchor Pottery Co., Trenton,
N. J. From 1894. Marks printed.

36, 37 Anna Pottery, Lowell, Ill. Marks
inscribed.

38, 39 Armstrong & Wentworth, Norwich, Conn. 1814-28. Impressed.

40 Avon Pottery, Cincinnati, Ohio.
Established 1886.

41 Baum, J. H., Wellsville, Ohio. 1880-
95. Printed.

42 Beech, Ralph B., Philadelphia, Pa.
Established 1845. Impressed.

UNITED STATES

JOHN BELL
4

JOHN BELL
WAYNESBORO, PA.
5

1

J. BELL   JOHN BELL   JOHN W. BELL   JOHN BELL   JOSEPH BELL

6   7   8   WAYNESBORO   10

9

2. BELL   S. BELL   S B   S. BELL   SOLOMON BELL   BELL

11   12   13   STRASBURG, VA.   STRASBURG, VA.   16

                      14   15

5. BELL & SONS   UPTON BELL   THE BELL POTTERY CO   B P Co   BELL CHINA

17   WAYNESBORO, PA.   FINDLAY OHIO   F O   B P Cº

        18   19   20   Findlay, Ohio.

                                         21   22

United States (Cont'd)

1, 2 Beerbower, L. B. & Co., Elizabeth, N. J. From 1879. Impressed.

3 Beerbower & Griffen, Phoenixville, Pa. Established 1877.

4-7 Bell, John, Waynesboro, Pa. 1826-81. Impressed.

8, 9 Bell, John W., Waynesboro, Pa. 1881-95.

10 Bell, Joseph, Putnam, Ohio. 1827-1850. Impressed.

11 Bell, Peter, Jr. Hagerstown, Md. & Winchester, Va. c. 1800.

12, 13 Bell, Samuel, Strasburg, Va. 1843-52. Impressed.

14-16 Bell, Samuel and Solomon, Strasburg, Va. 1852-82. Impressed.

17 Bell, S. & Sons, Strasburg, Va. 1882-1908. Impressed.

18 Bell, Upton, Waynesboro, Pa. 1895-99. Impressed.

19-21 Bell Pottery Co., Findlay, Ohio.

22 Bellmark Pottery Co., Trenton, N. J. Established 1893.

UNITED STATES

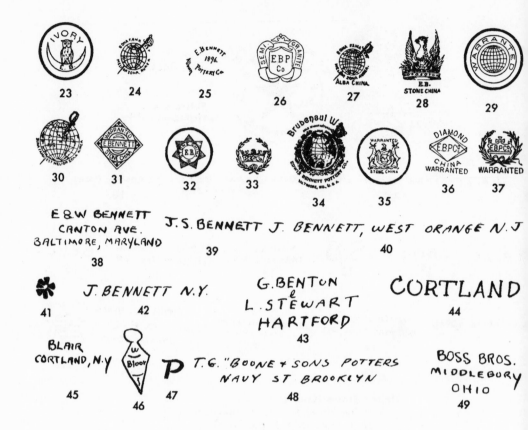

23 24 25 26 27 28 29

30 31 32 33 34 35 36 37

E & W BENNETT
CANTON AVE.
BALTIMORE, MARYLAND
38

J.S.BENNETT
39

J. BENNETT, WEST ORANGE N.J
40

J.BENNETT N.Y.
42

41

G.BENTON
&
L.STEWART
HARTFORD
43

CORTLAND
44

BLAIR
CORTLAND, N.Y
45

46

P
47

T.G. "BOONE & SONS POTTERS
NAVY ST BROOKLYN
48

BOSS BROS.
MIDDLEBURY
OHIO
49

23-37 Bennett, Edwin, Baltimore, Md.
From 1856-1890.
38 Bennett, E. & W., Baltimore, Md.
1848-56. Impressed.
39, 40 Bennett, James S. Moultonboro,
N. H. 1840-44. Impressed.
41 Bennett, James, about 1840. East
Liverpool, Ohio & Birmingham, Pa.
42 Bennett, John, New York City,
1876, West Orange, N. J., 1882.
43 G. Benton & L. Stewart about 1818.
44, 45 Blair, Sylvester, Cortland, N.Y.
1829-37. Impressed.
46 Bloor, William, 1862. Impressed.
47 Bonnin & Morris, Philadelphia, Pa.
1771-1772. Inscribed.
48 Boone, Thona, G. 1840-1846.
49 Boss Bros., Akron, Ohio. About
1874. Impressed.

UNITED STATES

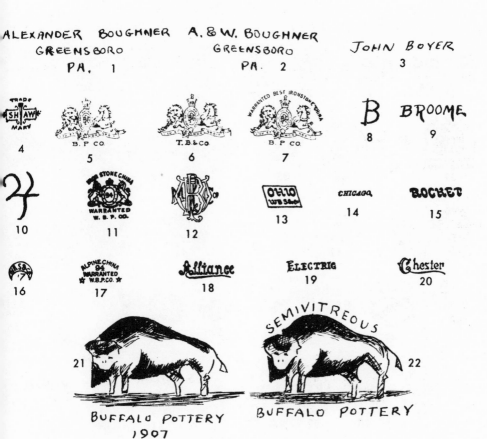

ALEXANDER BOUGHNER
GREENSBORO
PA. 1

A. & W. BOUGHNER
GREENSBORO
PA. 2

JOHN BOYER
3

4

B.P CO.
5

T.B.&CO.
6

WARRANTED BEST IRONSTONE CHINA
B.P CO.
7

B
8

BROOME
9

10

STONE CHINA
WARRANTED
W.B.P. CO.
11

12

OHIO
13

CHICAGO
14

ROCKET
15

16

ALPINE CHINA
WARRANTED
W.B.P.CO.
17

Alliance
18

ELECTRIC
19

Chester
20

21 BUFFALO POTTERY 1907

22 SEMIVITREOUS BUFFALO POTTERY

1 Boughner, Alexander, Greensboro, Pa. 1812-50. Impressed.

2 Boughner, A. & W., Greensboro, Pa. Impressed or in blue. 1850-90.

3 Boyer, John, Schuylkill Co., Pa. about 1810.

4 Bradshaw China Co., Niles, Ohio.

5-7 Brockman Pottery Co., Cincinnati, Ohio. Established 1862.

8-10 Broome, Isaac, Trenton, N. J. Established 1880.

11-20 William Brunt Pottery Co., E. Liverpool, Ohio. 1850-1894.

21, 22 Buffalo Pottery about 1905, Buffalo, N. Y.

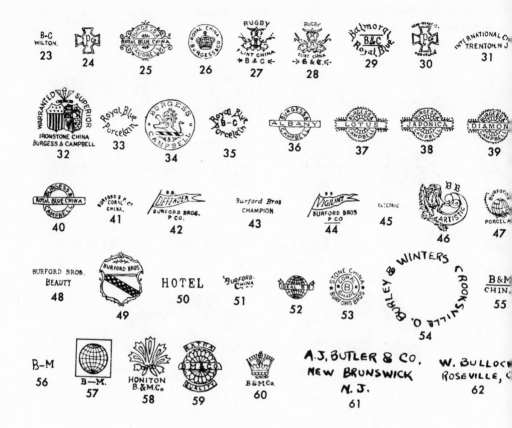

23-40 Burgess & Campbell (International Pottery Co.), Trenton, N. J. Established 1860.

41-53 Burford Bros. Pottery Co., E. Liverpool, Ohio. 1879-1900.

54 Burley & Winters, Crooksville, Ohio. After 1850.

55-60 Burroughs & Mountford, Trenton, N. J. 1879-1882.

61 Butler, A. J. & Co., New Brunswick, N. J. About 1850. Impressed.

62 Bullock, W., Roseville, Ohio, 1870-1885. Impressed.

UNITED STATES

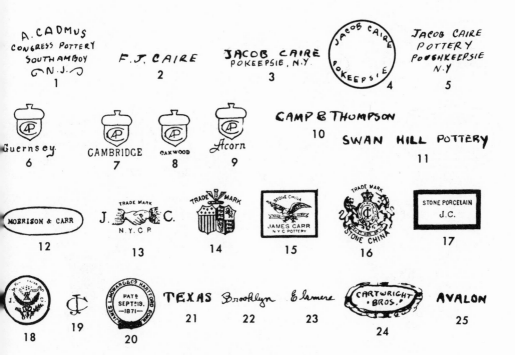

1 Cadmus, A., South Amboy, N. J.
About 1850. Impressed.
2 Caire, Frederick, J., Huntington, L. I.
1854-1863.
3-5 Caire, Jacob, Poughkeepsie, N. Y.
1842-1852. Impressed.
6-9 Cambridge Art Pottery Co., Cambridge, Ohio.
10 Camp & Thompson, Akron, Ohio.
c. 1870-1880. Impressed.
11 Carr, James, South Amboy, N. J.
1852-54. Impressed.
12-20 Carr & Morrison, (New York
City Pottery), New York, N. Y.
1853-88.
21-25 Cartwright Bros., E. Liverpool,
Ohio. 1880-1900.

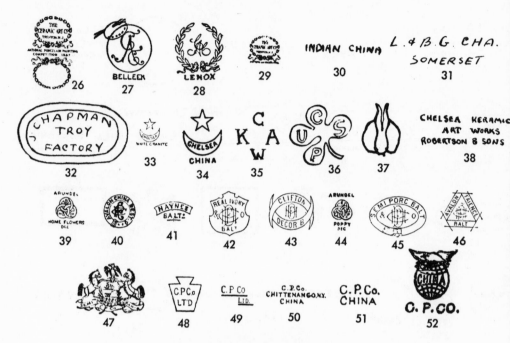

26-30 Ceramic Art Co. (Lenox) Trenton, N. J. Established 1889.

31 L. & B. G. Chase, Somerset, Mass. c. 1850. Impressed.

32 Chapman, J., Troy, N. Y. 1815-1820.

33, 34 Chelsea China Co., New Cumberland, W. Va. Established 1888-1893. Printed.

35-38 Chelsea Keramic Art Works, Chelsea, Mass. Established 1866. No. 35, impressed. No. 38, 1875-1889. No. 36, c. 1891. (J. Robertson & Sons).

39-46 Chesapeake Pottery Co., Baltimore, Md. Established 1880. F. Haynes & Co. From 1880-1890. Haynes, Bennett & Co. From 1890.

47-49 Chester Pottery Co., Phoenixville, Pa. Established 1894.

50-52 Chittenango Pottery Co., Chittenango, N. Y. Established 1897.

UNITED STATES

BENNETT & CHOLLAR
HOMER
1

CHOLLAR & DARBY
HOMER, N.Y.
2

3

KEZONTA
4

5

6

NATHAN CLARK or *NATHAN CLARK LYONS*
7   8

9

COLUMBIAN
TRENTON
N.J.
ART POTTERY
10

COMMERAW
11

COMMERAW'S
STONEWARE
NEW YORK
12

CORLEAR'S HOOK
13

COERLEARS
HOOK
N. YORK
14

BELLEEK

15   16   17

19

20   21   22

FHC
23

F.H.COWDEN
HARRISBURG
24

Cʰ H.C.
TRADE MARK
18

25

CALEB CRAFTS
26

1 Chollar & Bennett, Homer, N. Y. 1842-44. Impressed.

2 Chollar & Darby, Homer, N. Y. 1844-49. Impressed.

3-5 Cincinnati Art Pottery Co., Cincinnati, Ohio. Established 1879.

6 City Pottery Co., Trenton, N. J. Established 1859.

7, 8 Clark, Nathan, Athens, Lyons & Mt. Morris, N. Y. 1820-40 at Athens. 1850-90 at Lyons, Mark Impressed.

9, 10 Columbian Art Pottery, Trenton, N. J. Established 1876. (Morris & Willmore).

11, 12 Commeraw, Thomas, at Corlear's Hook, N. Y. c. 1802-20.

13, 14 Corlear's Hook, N. Y. c. 1800. Impressed. There are other variations of this mark.

15-22 Cook Pottery Co., Trenton, N. J. Established 1894-1900.

23-24 Cowden & Wilcox, Harrisburg, Pa. c. 1880. Impressed or in blue.

25 Coxon & Co., Trenton, N. J. 1863-1884. (Empire Pottery).

26 Crafts, Caleb, Portland, Me. 1837-1841. Impressed.

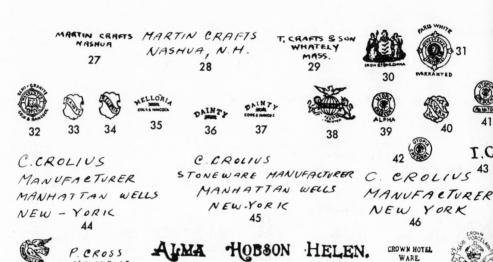

27, 28 Crafts, Martin, Nashua, N. H. 1845-1851. Impressed.

29 Crafts, Thomas & Elbridge. Whateley, Mass. 1820-48. Impressed.

30-42 Crescent Pottery Co. Trenton, N. J. Est. 1881.

43 Crolius, John, New York. Latter half 18th century. Impressed.

44, 45 Crolius, Clarkson, Sr. New York. About 1794-1837. Manhattan Wells probably not used after 1814.

46 Crolius, Clarkson, Jr. New York. 1838-1850.

47 Crooksville China Co. Crooksville, Ohio.

48 Cross, Peter. Hartford, Conn. 1805-1810.

49-55 Crown Pottery Co., Evansville, Ind. Est. 1891.

UNITED STATES

RENA. 1

IRONSTONE CHINA WARRANTED 2

C.P. CO. ROYAL 3

C.P. CO. REX 4

5

JEWEL C.P.Co 6

REGINA C.P. CO. 7

PAUL CUSHMAN 8

PAUL·CUSHMAN·STOE·WARE FACTORY·1809·HALF·A·MILE WEST OF ALBANY GOAL 9

DEDHAM POTTERY 10

11

UFGS 12

DELAWARE WARRANTED POTTERY 13

& WARRANTED 14

DENVER CT&P CO. 15

DENVER 16

DENVER (4F) 17 LONHUDA

DENVER (4F) LONHUDA 18

SUPERIOR CHINA CO. SEMI-GRANITE CHINA 19

JACOB DICK TUSCARAWAS CO. OHIO 20

J. DICK 21

C. DILLON & CO ALBANY 22

A.G.C. DIPPLE LEWISBURG, PA. 23

R. Drach 24

D 25

D. Dry 26

Columbus 27

DEWEY E.E.P.CO 28

EAST END P.CO E LIVERPOOL. O. 29

ROYAL IRONSTONE CHINA WARRANTED 30

Alaska 31

E.E.P.CO PORCELAIN 32

SEMI-VITREOUS PORCELAIN S A EAST LIVERPOOL POTTERIES CO. 33

PARIS WHITE D R 34

COLUMBIA 35

LAFAYETTE PORCELAIN 36

REVERE 37

IRONSTONE CHINA E.T.P.CO 38

E.T.P.CO. 39

IRONSTONE CHINA E.T.P.Co 40

STAR POTTERY 41

J.S. EBERLEY STRASBURG VA. 42

BARNABAS EDMUNDS + CO. CHARLESTOWN 43

EMPIRE TRENTON 44

EMPIRE POTTERY IRONSTONE CHINA A & M 45

IMPERIAL WARRANTED CHINA 46

1-7 Crown Pottery (Cont'd)

8, 9 Cushman, Paul. Albany, N. Y. 1805-1825. Impressed.

10-12 Dedham Pottery Co. Dedham, Mass. 1897.

13, 14 Delaware Pottery, Trenton, N. J. Established 1884.

15-18 Denver China & Pottery Co. Denver, Colo.

19 Derry China Co. Derry Station, Pa.

20, 21 Dick, Jacob. Tuscarawas County, Ohio. c. 1835. Impressed.

22 Dillon, C. & Co., Albany, N. Y. About 1835.

23 Dipple, A. G. Lewisburg, Pa. c. 1890. Impressed.

24 Drach, Rudolf, Bedminster, Pa. 1780-1800.

25 Dry, (Drey), John or Dry Bros. Dryville, Pa. 1804-c. 1850. Inscribed.

26 Dry Bros. from about 1850.

27-32 East End Pottery Co. E. Liverpool, Ohio.

33 East Liverpool Potteries Co., E. Liverpool, Ohio. From 1890.

34 East Morrisania China Works, New York, N. Y.

35-37 East Palestine Pottery Co. E. Palestine, Ohio.

38-40 East Trenton Pottery Co., Trenton, N. J. Established 1888.

41-42 Eberley, J. S., Strasburg, Va. 1880-1906. Impressed.

43 Edmunds, B. & Co. Charlestown, Mass. c. 1856. Impressed.

44-46 Empire Pottery, Trenton, N. J. 1863-1875. (Coxon & Co.)

UNITED STATES

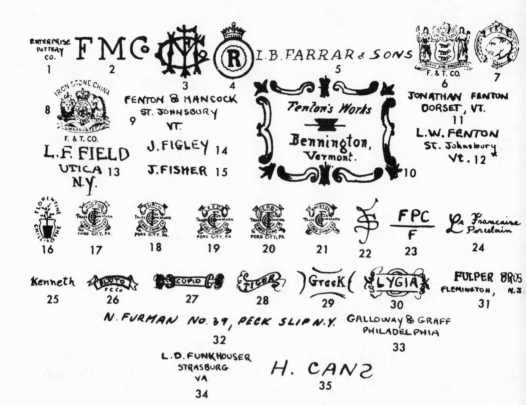

1 Enterprise Pottery, Trenton, N. J. Established 1880.

2-4 Faience Mfg. Co. Greenpoint, N. Y. 1880-1892. Printed.

5 Farrar, Isaac B. Fairfax, Vt. About 1798-1838.

6-8 Fell & Thropp Co. Trenton, N. J.

9 Fenton & Hancock, St. Johnsbury, Vt. (1859-1870). Impressed.

10 Fenton, C. W. Bennington, Vt. From about 1847 to 1849. Printed. Fenton, Hall & Co. (See Lyman, Fenton & Co.)

11 Fenton, Jonathan. Forset, Vt. 1801-1810. Impressed.

12 Fenton, L. W., St. Johnsbury, Vt. (1829-59). Impressed.

13 Field, L. F. Utica, N. Y. c. 1860-70.

14 Figley, Joseph. Newport, Ohio. c. 1850. Impressed.

15 Fisher, J. C. Hartford, Conn. 1805-12. Impressed.

16 Florentine Pottery Co., Chillicothe, Ohio.

17-21 Ford China Co., Ford City, Pa. Late 19th Century.

22 Frackleton, S. S. Milwaukee, Wis. Late 19th century.

23 Franklin Pottery Co., Franklin, Ohio. 1880-84. Impressed.

24 French China Co., Sebring, Ohio.

25-31 Fulper Bros. Flemington, N. J. 1805 through 19th cent. Impressed.

32 Furman, Noah, about 1840-1856. Cheesequake, N. J.

33 Funkhouser, L. D., Strasburg, Va. 1899-1905. Impressed.

34 Galloway & Graff, Philadelphia, Pa. Established 1868.

35 Gans, H. Lancaster County, Pa. about 1870.

UNITED STATES

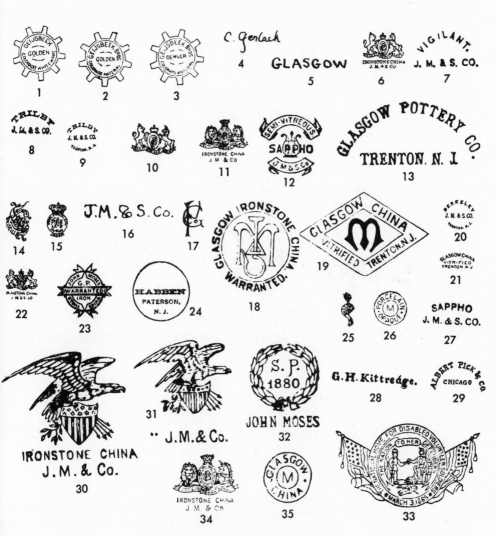

1-3 Geijsbeek Pottery Co., Golden, Colo. Established 1899.

4 Gerlach, C. Pennsylvania. Inscribed on redware.

5-35 Glasgow Pottery Co. (John Moses & Sons), Trenton, N. J. 1863-1890.

36 37 38 39 40

41 42 43 44

GOODWIN'S
HOTEL CHINA
45

46 47 48
GOODWIN BROS

SETH GOODWIN
49

T.O. GOODWIN
HARTFORD
50

GOODWIN & WEBSTER
51

36-41 Globe Pottery Co., E. Liverpool, Ohio. Established 1888. Successors to Frederick, Schenkle, Allen & Co. Established 1881.

42 Goodale, Daniel, Hartford, Conn. 1818-1830. Impressed.

43 Goodale & Stedman, Hartford, 1822.

44-48 Goodwin, John, E. Liverpool, Ohio. 1844-53. Printed. Succeeded by S. & W. Baggott. 1853-1895.

49 Goodwin, Seth. Hartford, Conn. 1795-1828.

50 Goodwin, Thomas O., Goodwin, Harvey, Hartford, Conn. 1820-1870.

51 Goodwin & Webster, Hartford, Conn. 1810-50. Impressed.

UNITED STATES

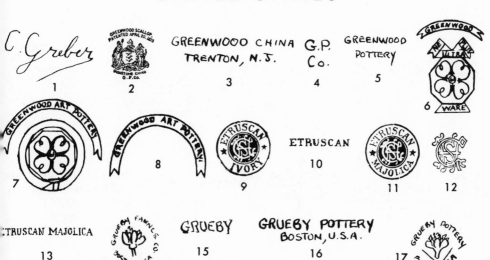

1 Greber Pottery, Upper Hanover,
Montgomery County, Pa. 1848-1855.

2-8 Greenwood Pottery (Stephens &
Tams), Trenton, N. J. Established
1861. Mark printed. Porcelain made
after 1876.

9-13 Griffen, Smith & Hill, Phoenixville, Pa. Established 1879-1890. Impressed and printed.

14-18 Grueby Faience Co., Boston,
Mass. Established 1897

19 Haig, Thomas, Philadelphia, Pa.
1812-1833.
Hall, E. (See W. P. Harris).

20 Hamilton & Jones, Greensboro, Pa.
c. 1870. Impressed or in blue.

21 Hamilton, Clem, Tuscarawas County, Ohio. c. 1870. Impressed.

22, 23 Hamilton, James (Eagle Pottery), Greensboro, Pa. 1844 to about
1890. Impressed or in blue.

24 Hamlyn, George, Bridgeton, N. J.
c. 1835. Impressed.

UNITED STATES

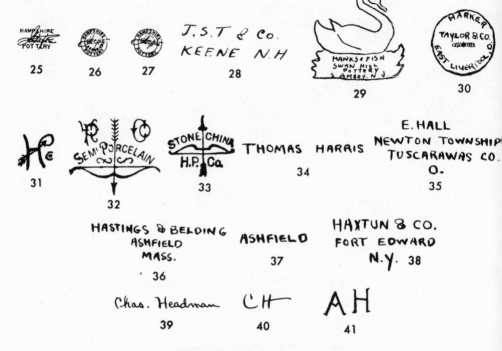

25   26   27

J.S.T & Co.
KEENE N.H
28

29

30

31   32   33   THOMAS HARRIS
34

E.HALL
NEWTON TOWNSHIP
TUSCARAWAS CO.
O.
35

HASTINGS & BELDING
ASHFIELD
MASS.
36

ASHFIELD
37

HAXTUN & CO.
FORT EDWARD
N.Y. 38

Chas. Headman
39

CH
40

AH
41

25-28 Hampshire Pottery Co. (J. S. Taft & Co.), Keene, N. H. Established 1871.

29 Hanks & Fish, Swan Hill Pottery, South Amboy, N. J. 1849.

30-33 Harker Pottery Co., E. Liverpool, Ohio. From 1890. Marks printed and in relief. #30, Harker, Taylor & Co., existed 1847-51. This mark in relief. (George S. Harker & Co. 1851-90).

34 Harris, Thomas, Cuyahoga Falls, Ohio. Established 1863. Impressed.

35 Harris, W. P., Newton, Tuscarawas, Ohio. 1828-56. Impressed.

36, 37 Hastings & Belding, Ashfield, Mass. 1850-54. Impressed.

38 Haxton & Co., Ft. Edward, N. Y. Established 1875. Impressed.

39 Headman, Andrew, Rock Hill, Pa. 1806-1840.

40, 41 Headman, Charles, Rock Hill, Pa. 1840-70.

UNITED STATES

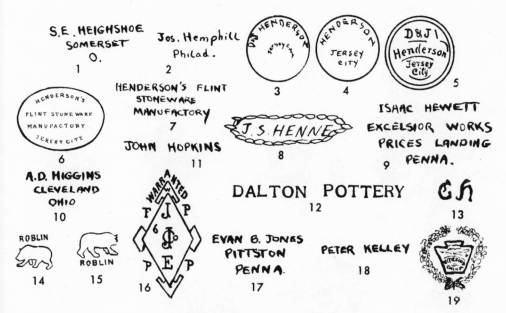

1 Heighshoe, S. E., Somerset, Ohio. c. 1850. Impressed.

2 Hemphill, Joseph, Philadelphia, Pa. 1833-38. Painted in red.

3-7 D. & J. Henderson, Jersey City, N. J. 1829-33. Marks impressed.

8 Henne, J. S., Shartlesville, Pa. About 1800. Impressed.

9 Hewitt, Isaac, Prices Landing, Pa. 1870-80. In blue.

10 Higgins, A. D. Cleveland, Ohio. 1837-50. Impressed.

11 Hopkins, John, Seneca County, Ohio. c. 1835. Impressed.

12 Houghton, Edwin (Dalton Pottery), Dalton, Ohio. 1864-1890. Impressed.

13 Hübener, George, Vincent, Pa. 1783-98.

14, 15 Irelan Linna, San Francisco, Calif. Established 1899.

16 Jeffords, J. E. & Co., Philadelphia, Pa. 1868-90. Printed.

17 Jones, Evan B., Pittston, Pa. c. 1880. Impressed.

18 Kelley, Peter, Philadelphia, Pa. c. 1840. Impressed.

19 Keystone Pottery Co., Trenton, N. J.

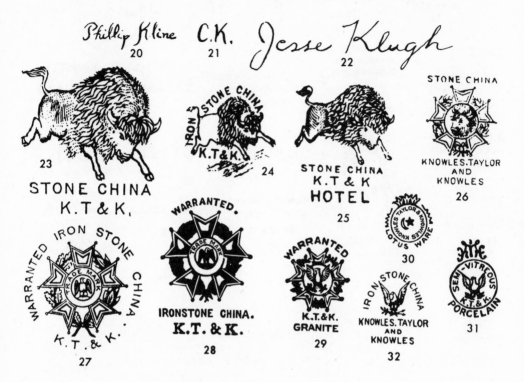

20 Kline, Phillip, Carversville, Pa. c. 1808.

21 Klinker, Christian, Bucksville, Pa. About 1772-92.

22 Klugh, Jesse, Morgantown, Pa. 1874.

23-32 Knowles, Taylor & Knowles, E. Liverpool, Ohio. From 1870.

UNITED STATES

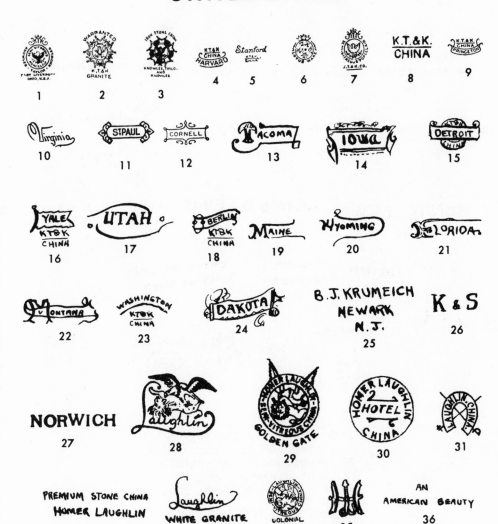

1-24 Knowles, Taylor & Knowles (Cont'd).

25 Krumeich, B. J., Newark, N. J. c. 1845-60. Impressed.

26 Kurlbaum & Schwartz, Philadelphia, Pa. c. 1853. Impressed.

27 Lathrop, Charles, Norwich, Conn. c. 1792. Impressed.

28-36 Homer Laughlin China Co., E. Liverpool, Ohio. Established 1874. Printed.

LEHEW & CO.
STRASBURG, VA.
37

W. H. Lehew & Co
Strasburg. VA
38

LOUIS LEHMAN
39

MADE·BY·J·LETTS
40

LEHMAN + RIEDINGER
41

Johannes
Leman
42

43 ❀ HENRY LEWIS
44

LEWIS & LEWIS
45

LEWIS & GARDINER
HUNTINGTON, L.I.
46 ᶾ

C.LINK
47

C.LINK
EXETER
48

CHRISTIAN LINK
STONETOWN
49

LONHUDA
50

LONHUDA
51

52

LONHUDA
LF
53

37-38 Lehew & Co., Strasburg, Va. Established 1885. Impressed.
39 Lehman, Louis, Poughkeepsie,N.Y. 1852-56. Impressed.
40 Letts, Joshua, Cheesequake, N. J. 1810-1815.
41 Louis, Lehman & Philip Riedinger, Poughkeepsie, N. Y. 1855.
42, 43 Leman, Johannes, Tyler's Port, Pa. c. 1830.
44 Lewis, Henry, Huntington, N. H. Before 1827. Impressed.
45 Lewis & Lewis, Huntington, N. Y. 1854-63. Impressed.
46 Lewis & Gardiner, Huntington, N. Y. 1827-1854. Impressed.
47-49 Link, Christian, Stonetown, Pa. From 1870. Impressed.
50-53 Lonhuda Pottery, Steubenville, Ohio. Established 1892.

UNITED STATES

1

J & J G. LOW,
PATENT
ART TILE WORKS
CHELSEA
MASS. U.S.A.
COPYRIGHT 1881 BY J & J G. LOW
2

E Lycett
3

4

J.M. MADDEN
RONDOUT
N.Y.
5

6

7

8

9

10

M
CHINA
L
11

WARRANTED

COAL PORT
TRENTON N.J.
12

COAL PORT
TRENTON. N.J.
13

JOHN MANN
RAHWAY
N.J.
14

MARKELL, IMMON & CO.
AKRON
O.   15

W. MARTEEN
16

1, 2 Low Art Tile Co., Chelsea, Mass.
Established 1887-1888.

3 Lycett, Edward, Atlanta, Ga. Established 1890.

4 Lyman, Fenton & Co., Bennington,
Vt. 1849-58. Printed. U. S. Pottery
from 1852. (Also see Norton or
Fenton).

5 Madden, J. M., Rondout, N. Y. c.
1870. Impressed.

6, 7 Thomas Maddock & Sons, Trenton, N. J. Established 1882.

8 Thomas Maddock's Sons Co., Trenton, N. J. From 1902.

9-11 Maddock Pottery Co., Trenton,
N. J. From 1893.

12, 13 John Maddock & Sons, Trenton, N. J. From 1894.

14 Mann, John, Rahway, N. J. Established 1830. Impressed.

15 Markell, Immon & Co., Akron,
Ohio. c. 1869. Impressed.

16 Marteen, W., Pennsylvania. c. 1875.
Impressed.

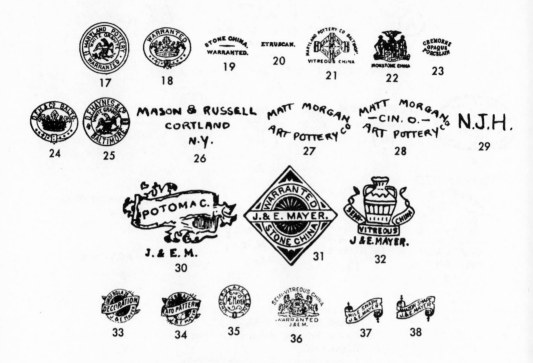

17-25 Maryland Pottery Co. (D. F. Haynes & Co.), Baltimore, Md. Established 1879.

26 Mason & Russel, Cortland, N. Y. c. 1870. Impressed.

27-29 Matt Morgan Art Pottery Co., Cincinnati, Ohio. Established 1883.

30-38 Mayer Pottery Co., Beaver Falls, Pa. Established 1881.

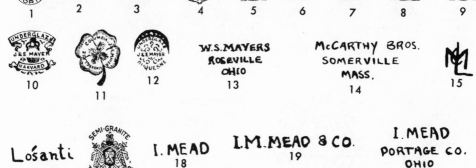

1-12 Mayer Pottery Co., (Cont'd).
13 Mayers, W. S., Roseville, Ohio. c. 1870. In blue.
14 McCarthy Bros., Somerville, Mass. c. 1870. Impressed.
15, 16 McLaughlin, M. L., Cincinnati, Ohio. Established 1876.
17 D. E. McNichol Pottery Co., E. Liverpool, Ohio. From 1892.
18-20 I. M. Mead & Co., Atwater, Ohio. c. 1850. Impressed.
21 Mear, Frederick, Boston, Mass. c. 1840. Impressed.
22 Medinger, Jacob, Neiffer, Pa. c. 1880-1930.
23 Mellick, H. H., Roseville, Ohio. c. 1875. Impressed.

UNITED STATES

LUZERNE
M.C
24

Nassau.
25

TACOMA
M
T
26

MERCER
SEMI VITREOUS
27

MERCER
28

M.C
Co.
29

Co.
WARRANTED
IRONSTONE
CHINA
30

WARRANTED · SUPERIOR.
IRONSTONE CHINA
MERCER POTTERY CO
31

MERCER
WARRANTED
CHINA
32

WALDORF
MERCER CHINA
33

SEMI·VITREOUS
ARDMORE
MERCER CHINA
35

Bordeaux
Mercer
34

SEMI·VITREOUS
TRINIDAD
MERCER CHINA
36

STONE CHINA
MERCER POTTERY CO.
37

MORAVIAN
M
38

MORAVIAN
39

E.H. MERRILL
SPRINGFIELD
O.
40

MERRIMAC
41

MERRIMAC
CERAMIC
COMPANY
42

24-37 Mercer Pottery Co., Trenton, N. J. Established 1868-69.
38, 39 Mercer, Henry C., (Moravian Pottery & Tile Works), Doylestown, Pa. c. 1890.
40 Merrill, Edwin H., Springfield, Ohio. c. 1835. Impressed.
41, 42 Merrimac Ceramic Co., Newburyport, Mass. Established 1897.

UNITED STATES

1, 2 Middle Lane Pottery, E. Hampton, N. Y. about 1890.

3, 4 Millington, Astbury & Poulson, Trenton, N. J. 1859-70.

5 Miner, William, Symmes Creek, Ohio. c. 1869. Impressed.

6 Monmouth Pottery Co., Monmouth, Ill. About 1890.

7 Morris & Willmore, Trenton, N. J. (See Columbia Art). Established 1876.

8 Mosaic Tile Co., Zanesville, Ohio.

9 Morgan, D., New York, N. Y. c. 1794-1804. Impressed.

10-13 George C. Murphy Pottery Co., E. Liverpool, Ohio.

14 Myers & Hall, Mogadore, Ohio. c. 1873. Impressed.

15 E. & G. Nash, Utica, N. Y. About 1820. Impressed.

16 New Castle Pottery Co., New Castle, Pa.

17-48 Newcomb Pottery, New Orleans, La. Established 1896. #23-48 are decorators marks.

49-57 New England Pottery Co., Boston, Mass. Established 1875. #49— Printed mark, 1878-1883. #50—c. 1880. #51—c. 1886-88. #52—c. 1886. #53—1883-1886. #54—c. 1887. #57—1888-89. #56—1889-95.

UNITED STATES

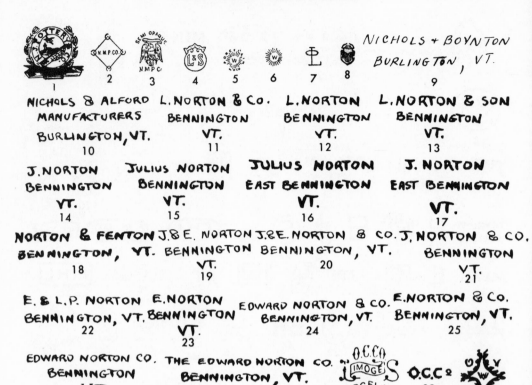

1 New Jersey Pottery Co., Trenton, N. J. 1869-1883.

2-8 New Milford Pottery Co., New Milford, Conn. Established 1886.

9 Nichols & Boynton, Burlington, Vt. c. 1856. Impressed.

10 Nichols & Alford, Burlington, Vt. c. 1854-1856.

11, 12 Norton, Luman, Bennington, Vt. #11—1823-28. #12—1828-33. Both Impressed.

13 L. Norton & Son, Bennington, Vt. 1833-40. Impressed.

14-17 Julius Norton, Bennington, Vt. (1841-44) (1847-50). Impressed.

18 Norton & Fenton, Bennington, Vt. 1844-47. Impressed.

19 J. & E. Norton, Bennington, Vt. 1850-59. Impressed.

20 J. & E. Norton Co., Bennington, Vt. 1859-61. Impressed.

21. J. Norton & Co., Bennington, Vt. 1859-61. Impressed.

22 E. & L. P. Norton, Bennington, Vt. 1861-81. Impressed.

23 Edward Norton, Bennington, Vt. 1881-83. Impressed.

24-27 Edward Norton & Co., Bennington, Vt. 1883-94. Impressed. #27—1886-94.

28, 29 Ohio China Co., E. Palestine, Ohio.

30 Ohio Valley China Co., Wheeling, W. Va. 1890-95.

UNITED STATES

O.V.
1

O V.
2

Biloxi
3

G.E.OHR, BILOXI
4

THE OLIVER CHINA CO.
SEBRING, O.
5

VERUS PORCELAIN
6

IRONSTONE CHINA O. P. Co
7

O.P.CO. SYRACUSE CHINA
8

9

10

O. P. Co. CHINA.
11

CHINA O.P.Co
12

ORCUTT, BELDING & Co. ASHFIELD MASS.
14

ORCUTT, GUILDFORD & Co. ASHFIELD, MASS.
15

O.P.Co. IMPERIAL
13

WALTER ORCUTT & Co. ASHFIELD, MASS.
16

ORCUTT, HUMISTON & Co. TROY, N.Y.
17

OTT & BREWER Co TRENTON
18

BELLEEK O&B
19

BELLEEK & Co TRENTON
20

21

O. B. CHINA
22

ROYAL CROWN ETRURIA
23

ETRURIA STONE CHINA
24

O. & B.
25

SEMI WARRANTED PORCELAIN
26

ETRURIA CHINA POTTERY Co
27

WARRANTED IRONSTONE CHINA
28

MANUFACTURED BY OTT & BREWER TRENTON N.J USA
29

OTT & BREWER CO BELLEEK
30

O&B
31

BELLEEK
32

OWENS UTOPIAN
33

HENRI DEUX
34

OWENS FEROZA
35

1, 2 Ohio Valley China Co. (Cont'd).

3, 4 Ohr, George E. Biloxi, Miss. 1890-1900.

5, 6 Oliver China Co., Sebring, Ohio. Established 1899.

7-13 Onondaga Pottery Co., Syracuse, N. Y. Established 1871.

14 Orcutt, Belding & Co., Ashfield, Mass. 1848-50. Impressed.

15 Orcutt, Guildford & Co., Ashfield, Mass. 1848-50. Impressed.

16 Walter Orcutt & Co., Ashfield, Mass. 1848-50. Impressed.

17 Orcutt, Humiston & Co., Troy, N. Y. c. 1850-60. Impressed.

18-32 Ott & Brewer, Trenton, N. J. 1867-92. The word "BELLEEK" was included in the mark from about 1882. #32—about 1867.

33-35 J. B. Owens Pottery Co., Zanesville, Ohio. 1885-92.

UNITED STATES

1 Paul, Samuel, Pennsylvania.
2, 3 Pauline Pottery, Edgerton, Wis.
Established 1883. #2—Impressed
on early pieces. Printed on later
wares. #3—about 1888.
4 Penna. Museum & School of In-
dustrial Art. Established 1903.
5-7 Pen Yan Pottery, Yates County,
N. Y. about 1830-1850.
8-15 Peoria Pottery Co., Peoria, Ill.
1873-94.
16, 17 Perry, Mary C., Detroit, Mich.
18 Peyrau, A., New York City, 1891.
19 Phoenix Pottery, Phoenixville, Pa.
Established 1867.
20-28 Pioneer Pottery Co., Wellsville,
Ohio. 1885-1896. #21 & 22—Morley & Co. 1879-1885.

UNITED STATES

PFALTZGRAFF POTTERY

29

30

DRESDEN
HOTEL CHINA
WARRANTED
31

DRESDEN
SEMI-PORCELAIN
32

DRESDEN
HOTEL CHINA.
33

DRESDEN
VITREOUS
PORCELAIN
EAST LIVERPOOL, O.
34

DRESDEN
WHITE-GRANITE
35

YALE
36

DRESDEN STONE CHINA.
37

DRESDEN
WARRANTED
CHINA
38

Dresden
39

California
40

Madrid
41

MADE by XERXES
PRICE S. AMBOY
42

XF
43

D__D
44

IRONSTONE CHINA
I. DAVIS
45

PATENTED AUG 26th '79.
I DAVIS.
46

PORCELAINE OPAQUE
I DAVIS
47

IRON-
STONE CHINA
DALE & DAVIS.
48

29 Pfaltzgraff Pottery, York, Pa. c.
1840-1900. Impressed.

30 C. & H. Poillon, Woodbridge,
N. J.

31-41 Potters Cooperative Co., E.
Liverpool, Ohio. Established 1892.
Brunt, Bloor & Martin from 1875.

42, 43 Price, Xerxes, Sayreville, N. J.
About 1802. Impressed.

44-48 Prospect Hill Pottery Co., Trenton, N. J. Established 1880.

UNITED STATES

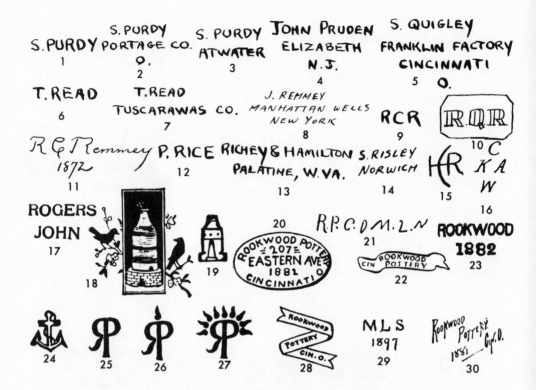

1-3 Purdy, Solomon, Atwater, Ohio. c. 1820. Impressed.

4 Pruden, John, Elizabeth, N. J. About 1830-76. Impressed.

5 Quigley, S.,Cincinnati,Ohio. c. 1834. This mark questionable.

6, 7 Read, Thomas, Newport, Ohio. 1850-1865. Impressed.

8 Remmey, John III, New York, N. Y. 1799-1814. On brown stoneware. Impressed.

9-11 Remmey, Richard C., Philadelphia, Pa. Established about 1859. Impressed.

12 Rice, Prosper, Putnam, Ohio. 1827-1850. Impressed.

13 Richey & Hamilton, Palatine, W. Va. c. 1875. Mark in blue.

14 Risley, Sidney, Norwich, Conn. About 1836. Impressed.

15, 16 Robertson Art Tile Co., Morrisville, Pa.

17 Rogers, John, New York, N. Y. About 1860 to 1890. Terra cotta figures and groups.

18-30 Rookwood Pottery, Cincinnati, Ohio.Established 1879. #26—1881-1883. #27 — 1886. #28 — 1887. #29—1895. #27-29 are generally impressed. A dot was added yearly after 1886.

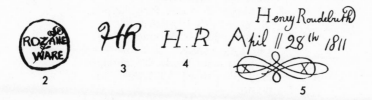

1 Rookwood (Cont'd). Marks of Rookwood decorators. 1904.
2 Roseville Pottery, Zanesville, Ohio.
3-5 Roudebuth, Henry. Montgomery Co., Pa. Early 19th century.

UNITED STATES

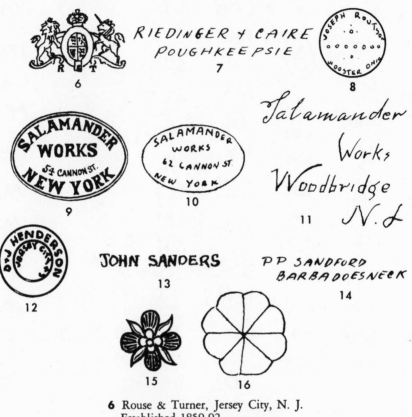

6 Rouse & Turner, Jersey City, N. J. Established 1859-92.

7 Riedinger & Caire, Poughkeepsie, N. Y. 1856-78. Impressed.

8 Routson, Joseph, Wooster, Ohio. . Late 19th century.

9-12 Salamander Works, Woodbridge, N. J. Established 1825-1896. Impressed.

13 John Sanders, Connecticut. c. 1817.

14 Sandford, P. P. (Barbadoes Neck) now Hackensack, N. J. 18th Century.

15, 16 School, Michael, Tylersport, Montgomery Co. Pa. About 1830. Impressed.

UNITED STATES

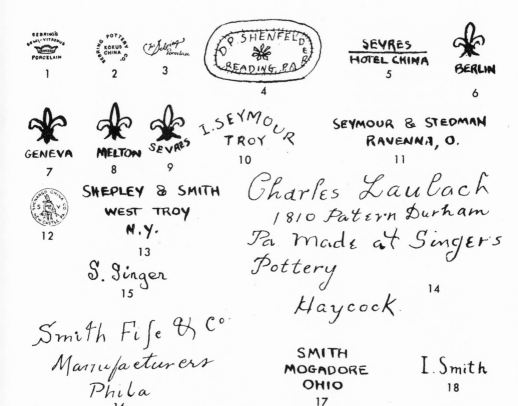

1. SEBRING'S SEMI-VITREOUS PORCELAIN

2. SEBRING POTTERY KOKUS CHINA CO.

3. Jno. Sebring Porcelain

4. D. P. SHENFELDER READING, PA

5. SEVRES HOTEL CHINA

6. BERLIN

7. GENEVA

8. MELTON

9. SEVRES

10. I. SEYMOUR TROY

11. SEYMOUR & STEDMAN RAVENNA, O.

12. SHENANGO CHINA S V Co NEW CASTLE PA

13. SHEPLEY & SMITH WEST TROY N.Y.

14. Charles Laubach 1810 Patern Durham Pa Made at Singer's Pottery Haycock

15. S. Singer

16. Smith Fife & Co Manufacturers Phila

17. SMITH MOGADORE OHIO

18. I. Smith

1-3 Sebring Pottery Co., Sebring, Ohio. Established 1887.

4 Shenfelder, Daniel P., Reading, Pa. Established 1869. Impressed.

5-9 Sevres China Co., E. Liverpool, Ohio. Established 1900.

10 Seymour, Israel, Troy, N.Y. c. 1809-52. Impressed.

11 Seymour & Stedman, Ravenna, Ohio. c. 1850. Impressed.

12 Shenango China Co., New Castle, Pa.

13 Shepley & Smith, W. Troy, N.Y. About 1865-95. Impressed.

14, 15 Singer, Simon, Haycock, Pa. c. 1810.

16 Smith, Fife & Co. Philadelphia, Pa. 1830. Painted in red.

17 Smith, J. C., Mogadore, Ohio. c. 1862. Impressed.

18 Smith, Joseph, Wrightstown, Pa. 1763 to about 1800.

UNITED STATES

AMERICAN GIRL
19

Smith Phillips Semi Porcelain
20

KOSMO
21

22

FENIX
23

UNION PORCELAIN WORKS N.Y.
24

25

U.P.W.
26

UNION PORCELAIN WORKS GREENPOINT N.Y.
27

UNION PORCELAIN WORKS N Y
28

K.L.H MÜLLER 1875
29

SMITH
30

W.SMITH
31

WOMELSDORF
32

SOMERSET POTTERY WORKS
33

S P COMPANY KAOLIN S.C.
34

S.P. Co =
35

David Spinner
36

37

S.E.T. CO.
38

19-23 Smith-Phillips China Co., E. Liverpool, Ohio. Late 19th century.

24-29 Smith, Thomas C. & Sons (Union Porcelain Works), New York, N. Y. From about 1870. Marks shown are after 1876.

30-32 Smith, Willoughby, Womelsdorf, Pa. 1864-1905. Impressed.

33 Somerset Pottery Works, Somerset, Mass. c. 1875. Impressed.

34, 35 Southern Porcelain Co., Kaolin, S. C. 1856-64.

36 David Spinner, Melford, Pa. 1800-11.

37 Spoon Pottery, Berks Co. Pa. 19th Century.

38 Star Encaustic Tile Co., Pittsburgh, Pa. Established 1882.

1 Star Porcelain Co., Trenton, N. J. Established late 19th century.

2-15 Steubenville Pottery Co., Steubenville, Ohio. Established 1879.

16 Stockton Art Pottery Co., Stockton, Calif.

17 Stockwell, Henry, Columbian Factory, Perth Amboy, N. J. 1831.

18 Stofflet, Heinrich, Berks County, Pa. c. 1814.

19 Summit China Co., Akron, Ohio. c. 1890. Printed.

20 Hiram Swank & Sons, Johnstown, Pa. About 1865-1900. Impressed.

21, 22 Taney, Jacob, Nockamixon, Pa. c. 1794.

23-26 Taylor, Smith & Taylor Co., E. Liverpool, Ohio. Established 1899.

27, 28 Thomas China Co., Lisbon, Ohio.

29-35 C. C. Thompson Pottery Co., E. Liverpool, Ohio. Established 1868.

36 Tomlinson, Lewis K. Dryville, Pa. c. 1850-1889. Impressed or inscribed.

UNITED STATES

TRENTON CHINA CO.
TRENTON, N.J.

1

2

3

TRENTON POTTERIES CO.
TRENTON, NEW JERSEY
USA

4

T P.Co
CHINA

5

6

7

8

9

10

11

T.P.Co.
CHINA

12

SEMI-GRANITE.

13

TRENT TILE
TRENTON, N.J
U.S.A &

15

Samuel Troxel
Potter 1825

16

FRENCH
T.P.W.

14

S.T.P.
1824

17

William Ellis Tucker
China Manufacturer
Philadelphia
1828

18

Tucker & Hulme
Philadelphia
1828

19

Tucker & Hulme
China Manufacturers
Philadelphia
1828

20

1 Trenton China Co., Trenton, N. J.
1859-1891.

2-11 Trenton Potteries Co., Trenton,
N. J. Established 1865.

12 Trenton Pottery Co., Trenton, N. J.
Established 1852. This mark used
1865 to 1872.

13, 14 Trenton Pottery Works, Trenton, N. J. Late 19th century.

15 Trenton Tile Co., Trenton, N. J.
1885.

16, 17 Troxel, Samuel, Troxel Pottery,
Montgomery Co. Pa. 1823-1833.

18 Tucker, W. E. Philadelphia, Pa.
From about 1826. Painted over-glaze.

19, 20 Tucker & Hulme, Philadelphia,
Pa. 1828.

UNITED STATES

21

22

C.TUPPER
PORTAGE CO.
O.

23

24

25

26

27

Raleigh

28

The Admiral

29

Champion

30

31

32

33

21, 22 Hemphill, Joseph, Philadelphia, Pa. 1832-1836.
23 Tupper, C., Portage County, Ohio. c. 1870. Impressed.
24-27 Union Potteries Co., E. Liverpool, Ohio. Latter half 19th Century.
28-30 United States Pottery, E. Liverpool, Ohio. Latter half 19th Century.
31-33 United States Pottery (O. A. Gager & Co.), Bennington, Vt. 1852-1858.

UNITED STATES

UNITED STATES

A.Weaver

1

J.A.Weber

2

M.C. WEBSTER + SON
HARTFORD

3

WEBSTER + SEYMOUR
HARTFORD

4

WEEKS, COOK, & WEEKS

5

Aurelian
WELLER

6

DICKENS WARE
WELLER.

7

Eosian
WELLER

8

DICKENS
WELLER

9

TURADA
WELLER

10

LOUWELSA
WELLER

11

Liberty

12

W.S.Co.
SEMI-PORCELAIN

13

IMPERIAL CHINA

14

MORLEY & CO.
MAJOLLICA
WELLSVILLE, O.

15

W P P Co
SEMI-PORCELAIN

16

M & CO.
IRON STONE CHINA

17

PORCELAIN
P.P.
WORKS
CHINA

18

P P W C

19

1 Weaver, Abraham, Nockamixon, Pa. 1824-44.

2 Weber, J. A. Barnesville, Pa. c. 1875. Impressed.

3 Webster, M. C. & Son, Hartford, Conn. 1840-57. Impressed.

4 Webster & Seymour. Hartford, Conn. 1857-73. Impressed.

5 Weeks, Cook & Weeks, Akron, Ohio. From 1882.

6-11 Weller, S. A., Zanesville, Ohio. Late 19th century.

12-19 Wellsville China Co., Wellsville, Ohio. Established 1879.

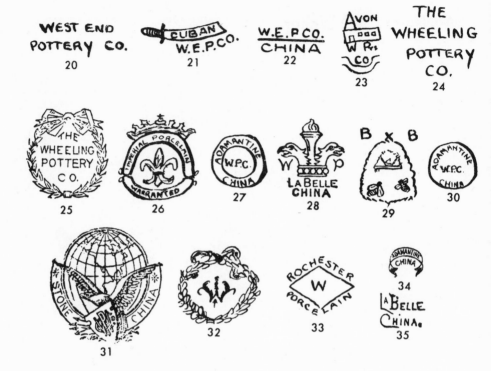

20-22 West End Pottery Co., E. Liverpool, Ohio. Established 1893.

23 Wheeling Potteries Co., Wheeling, W. Va. Established 1903.

24-35 Wheeling Pottery Co., Wheeling, W. Va. Established 1879.

UNITED STATES

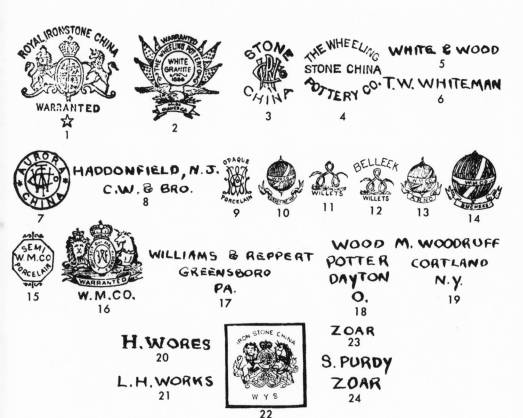

1-4 Wheeling Pottery Co. (Cont'd).

5 White & Wood, Binghamton, N. Y. c. 1855. Impressed.

6 Whiteman, T. W., Perth Amboy, N. J. c. 1863. Impressed.

7 Wick China Co., Kittanning, Pa.

8 Wingender, Chas. & Brother, Haddonfield, N. J. c. 1890. Impressed.

9-16 Willetts Mfg. Co., Trenton, N. J. Established 1879.

17 Williams & Reppert, Greensboro, Pa. c. 1875. Impressed or in blue.

18 Wood, Dayton, Ohio. c. 1870. Impressed.

19 Woodruff, Madison, Cortland, N.Y. 1849 to about 1870. Impressed.

20 Wores, H., Dover, Ohio. About 1825-46. Impressed.

21 Works, Laban H., Newport, Ohio. c. 1845. Impressed.

22 William Young & Sons, Trenton, N. J. Established 1853.

23, 24 Zoar Pottery, Zoar, Ohio. About 1834-50. Impressed.

INDEX

159

Butler, Edward, 73
Butts, Rivett & Heath, 54

Cabau, 20
Cadmus, A., 121
Caen, 4
Caffaggiolo, 89
Caire, Frederick J., 121
Caire, Jacob, 121
Caldas, 109
Calland, J. F., 73
Cambrian Pottery, 72
Cambridge Art Pottery Co., 121
Camp & Thompson, 121
Campbell, C. M., 67, 69
Campini, F., 102
Cantagalli, 94
Capelle, 16
Capelletti, 90
Capo-di-Monte, 90, 91, 111, 112
Capronnier, 20
Cardin, 16
Cari, C., 104
Carlsbad, 28
Carl, Theodore, 32
Carocci, Fabbri & Co., 98
Carr & Morrison, 121
Carr, James, 121
Carrier, 16
Cartlidge, F. & Co., 61
Cartwright Bros., 121
Casa Pirota, 91, 92, 93
Casali & Caligari, 101
Case, Mort & Co., 60
Castel, 16
Castel-Durante, 90
Castelli, 90
Castleford, 59
Catherine II, 14, 110
Caton, 16
Catrice, 16
Caughley, 50-51, 52, 76
Cauldon, 65
Caussy, P., 12
Celos, 20

Ceramic Art Co., 122
Chabry, 16
Chace, L. & B. C., 122
Chaffers, Richard, 60
Chamberlain, R. & Son, 76, 78
Chamberlain, Walter, 78
Chambers, John, 83
Champion, 47, 64
Chanou, 16
Chanou, Henri F., 9
Chantilly, 5, 77
Chapel, S. & J., 59
Chapman, D., 61
Chapman, J., 122
Chapuis, 16
Charles III, 90, 111
Charlottenberg, 28
Charpentier, 20
Charrin, 20
Chauveaux, 16
Chelsea, 51, 52, 53, 78
Chelsea China Co., 122
Chelsea Derby, 51
Chelsea Keramic Art Co., 122
Chesapeake Pottery Co., 122
Chester Pottery Co., 122
Chetham & Wooley, 62
Chevalier, 16
Chicanneau, 10
Child, 74
China, 2, 63
Chiodo, 102
Chittenango Pottery Co., 122
Chmeloff, 108
Chodau, 28
Choisy, De, 16
Choisy le Roi, 5
Chollar & Bennett, 123
Chollar & Darby, 123
Christian, P., 60
Chulot, 16
Chur Bayera, 32
Church Gresley, 51
Ciañico, 90
Cincinnati Art Pottery Co., 123
City Pottery Co., 123

162

England (See Great Britain)
Enterprise Pottery, 126
Escallier, 21
Este, 91
Etiolles, 5
Etruria, 67, 75
Etterbeek, 1
Evans, 17
Evans & Co., 72
Evans & Glasson, 72, 73
Evans, D. J. & Co., 73
Ewar, The, 85

Fabriano, 91
Faenza, 91-94
Faience Mfg. Co., 126
Falconet, 17
Falot, 17
Fanciullacci, 91
Faraguet, 21
Farini, A., 91, 94
Farnsworth, I., 54
Farrar, J. B., 126
Fauchier, 7
Fell and Thropp, 126
Fell, T. & Co., 64
Fenton, 55-56, 67, 80
Fenton & Hancock, 126
Fenton, C. W., 126
Fenton, Hall & Co., 126
Fenton, Jonathan, 126
Fenton, L. W., 126
Ferdinand IV, 90
Ferguson, Miller & Co., 83
Fernex, 17
Feuillet, 10
Ficquenet, 21
Field, L. F., 126
Fife Pottery, 83
Figley, Jos., 126
Fischer & Mieg, 39
Fischer & Reichembach, 38
Fischer, Christian, 38
Fischer, Moritz, 33
Fischern, 31

Fisher, J. C., 126
Fletcher, T. & Co., 65
Flight, 78
Flight & Barr, 78
Flight, Barr & Barr, 76, 78
Flight, John and Jos., 76
Flight, Thomas, 76
Florence, 91, 94
Florentine Pottery Co., 126
Florida, 112
Flörsheim, 31
Flower, Jos., 47
Flowerpot, The, 85
Foley China Works, 56
Fontaine, 17, 21
Fontainebleu, 5, 9
Fontana, O. & F., 103
Fontebasso, 103
Fontelliau, 17
Ford, Charles, 80
Ford China Co., 126
Ford Pottery, 71
Forli, 95
Fortling, J., 3
Fortune, The, 86
Fouque, Arnoux & Co., 24
Four Roman Heroes, The, 86
Fouré, 17
Fournier, 21
Fowke, F. G., 62
Fowler, Thompson & Co., 84
Frackleton, S. S., 126
Fragonard, 21
Frain, 38
France, 4-25
Franchini, G., 91
Franke, A., 43
Frankenthal, 31, 32, 33
Frankfort, 38
Franklin Pottery Co., 126
Frantzen, 113
Frede, J. C., 35
Frederick, V., 3
Frederick, Schenkle, Allen & Co., 128
Freiburg, 43
French China Co., 126

Greenwood Pottery, 129
Greenwood, S., 55
Greinstadt, 33
Gremont, 17
Griffin, Smith & Hill, 129
Grimwade Bros., 70
Grison, 17
Grohn, 33
Grossbreitenbach, 33
Grosvenor & Son, 84
Grue, F. A., 100
Grueby Faience Co., 129
Grunstadt, 33
Gubbio, 96-98
Guerhard, 9
Guidobono, B., 102
Guillebaud, 12
Guillemain, 21
Gulina, M., 110
Gustafsberg, 113
Guy & Housel, 10

Haager, Horth & Co., 43
Haas, 41
Hackwood, 58, 65
Hadley, J. & Sons, 76, 79
Haguenau, 24
Haig, Thomas, 129
Hall, E., 130
Hallion, 21
Hamilton, Clem, 129
Hamilton, James, 129
Hamilton & Jones, 129
Hamlyn, George, 129
Hammann, 43
Hammersley & Co., 61
Hampshire Pottery Co., 130
Hancock, Sampson, 55
Hanks & Fish, 130
Hanley, 57-58, 67, 80
Hannong & Lemaire, 25
Hannong, 24, 25
Hannong, Joseph A., 31, 32
Hannong, Paul, 31, 32
Hannong, Pierre, 10, 24

Hanstein, 37
Hardin, Thomas, 83
Harding, W. & J., 65
Harker, G. S. & Co., 130
Harker Pottery Co., 130
Harker, Taylor & Co., 130
Harley, T., 62
Harris, Thomas, 130
Harris, W. P., 130
Hartley, Greens & Co., 59
Hastings & Belding, 130
Haviland & Co., 6
Hawkes, J. & Co., 83
Haxtun & Co., 130
Haynes, Bennett & Co., 122
Haynes, D. F. & Co., 122, 136
Haynes, George, 72
Headman, Andrew, 130
Headman, Charles, 130
Heath, J. & Co., 75
Heckman, A., 26
Heighshoe, S. E., 131
Hemphill, Jos., 131, 151
Henderson, D. & J., 131
Henne, J. S., 131
Henrion, 17
Henry II, 12
Herculaneum Pottery, 60
Herend, 33
Hericourt, 17
Herreboe, 107
Hesse-Cassel, 33
Hesse-Darmstadt, 34
Hewelke, 105
Hewitt, Isaac, 13
Hicks & Meigh, 65
Hicks, Meigh & Johnson, 65
Higgins, A. D., 131
Hildebrandt, F., 40
Hilditch & Hopwood, 61
Hilditch & Son, 61
Hilken, 17
Hill & Co., 61
Hills, Joseph, 54
Hirsch, 31
Hispano-Moresque, 112

Krause, M., 41
Kriegel & Co., 39
Krister, C., 35
Kronenburg, 36
Krumeich, B. J., 133
Kunersberg, 35
Kurlbaum & Schwartz, 133
Kutani, 106
Kuznetsoff, S. T., 110

La China, 111
La Fond, A. & Co., 84, 85
La Hubaudière & Co., 11
La Moncloa, 112
La Roche, 17
La Rochelle, 6
La Sienie, 6
La Tour d'Aigues, 6
Lakin & Poole, 58
Lambert, 21
Lambeth, 59
Lammens, B. & Co., 1
Landais, F. M., 24
Lane Delph, 59, 67
Lane End, 61, 67, 81
Lanfrey, F. C., 9
Langlacé, 21
Langlois, 21
Lassere, 21
Lassia, J. J., 10
Latache, 22
Latens & Rateau, 4
Lathrop, Charles, 133
Laughlin, H. China Co., 133
Lavalle, Dr. J., 11
Le Bel, 17, 22
Le Brun, Benoist, 9
Le François, M., 4
Le Guay, 22
Le Guay, E. H., 18
Le Gury, P. A., 18
Le Montet, 6
Le Nove, 90, 91, 98
Le Riche, 18
Le Tourneur, 18

Le Troune, 18
Leandre, 17
Leboeuf, A. M., 10
Lecot, 18
Ledoux, 18
Leeds, 59, 73
Leeds Pottery Co., 59
Lefebvre, Denis, 8
Legay, 22
Leger, 22
Legrand, 22
Lehew & Co., 134
Lehman, Lewis, 134
Lehman & Riedinger, 134
Leigh, G. & R., 52
Leigh, J. E., 48
Lemaire, 25
Leman, Johannes, 134
Lenz, F., 43
Leroy, 22
Lessore, Emile, 76
Lesum, 35
Lettin, 35
Letts, Joshua, 134
Levantino, L., 102
Leve, 18
Lewis, Henry, 134
Lewis & Gardner, 134
Lewis & Lewis, 134
Liance, 18
Liege, 1
Ligue, 22
Lille, 6
Lilly, J. & F., 76
Limbach, 33, 35, 36
Limerick, 83
Limoges, 6-7
Link, Christian, 134
Lippert & Haas, 41
Lisbon, 109
Liverpool, 60
Locke, Edward, 76, 79
Locker & Co., 54
Lockett, J. & G., 62
Lockett, J. & Sons, 62
Lodi, 99

168

Renard, E., 22
Renard, H., 22
Rendsburg, 40
Rheinsberg, 40
Rice, Prosper, 144
Richard, Emile, 22
Richard, Eugène, 22
Richard, F., 23
Richard, J. & Co., 100
Richard, L., 23
Richard, N., 23
Richard, P., 23
Richey & Hamilton, 144
Ridgway, 65, 66
Ridgway, Job, 65, 80
Ridgway, J. & Co., 65
Ridgway, J. & W., 65
Ridgway, Morley, Wear & Co., 56, 65
Ridgway, W., 65
Ridgway, W. & Son, 65
Riedinger, Philip, 134
Riedinger & Caire, 146
Riley, J. & R., 50
Rimini, 101
Riocreux, D., 23
Riocreux, I., 23
Risley, Sidney, 144
Rissler & Co., 43
Ristori, T. H., 7
Robb, W. & Co., 83
Robert, J., 23
Robert, J. G., 7
Robert, Mdme., 23
Robert, P., 23
Robertson Art Tile Co., 144
Robertson, J. & Sons, 122
Robinson & Son, 61
Rocher, 19
Rockingham, 73
Roger, 23
Rogers, 61
Rogers, John, 144
Roman, The, 87
Rome, 101
Rookwood Pottery, 144-145
Rörstrand, 113

Rosch, 34
Rose, John, 52
Rose, J. & Co., 50
Rose, The, 85, 88
Rosetti, 103
Roseville Pottery, 145
Rosset, 19
Rossetti, 90
Rotberg, 32
Roudebuth, Henry, 145
Rouen, 12
Rouse & Turner, 146
Roussel, 19, 23
Roussencq, J. P., 7
Rouston, Jos., 146
Rowley & Newton, Ltd., 61
Rubati, Pasquale, 100
Rubatto, S., 102
Rückingen, 40
Rudolstadt, 40
Rue de Bondy, 9
Rue de la Roquette, 11
Rue Fontaine au Roi, 11
Ruskin Pottery, 80
Russia, 110

Sadler & Green, 60
Sadler, John, 60
Saeltzer, A., 31
Sailly, N., 24
St. Amand les Eaus, 12
St. Antoine Faubourg, 9
St. Cloud, 12
St. Denis Faubourg, 10
St. Paul, 13
St. Petersburg, 110
St. Porchaire, 12
Salamander Works, 146
Salomone, G., 102
Salt, Ralph, 50
Sampson, Bridgwood & Son, 61
Samson, 11, 31
Sanders, John, 146
Sanders, William, 63
Sandford, P. P., 146

173

Warner, William E., 152
Warrilow, G. & Son, 61
Warsaw, 108
Warwick China Co., 152
Weatherby, J. H. & Sons, 57, 58
Weaver, Abraham, 153
Weber, J. A., 153
Webster & Seymour, 153
Webster, M. C. & Son, 153
Wedgwood, 34, 75-76
Wedgwood & Bentley, 75
Wedgwood, John, 75
Wedgwood, Josiah, 75
Wedgwood, Josiah, & Sons, Ltd., 75
Wedgwood, Ralph, 50, 72, 81
Wedgwood Thomas, 75
Weeks, Cook, & Weeks, 153
Weesp, 84, 85
Wegely, 26
Welby, F. L., 42
Weller, S. A., 153
Wellsville China Co., 153
Werdinger, 23
Wessel, M. L., 39
West End Pottery Co., 153
Wetherill, T., 59
Wexford, 83
Whalley, Smith & Skinner, 71
Wheeling Potteries Co., 154
Wheeling Pottery Co., 154-155
Whieldon, Thomas, 56
White & Wood, 155
Whiteman, T. W., 155
Whittaker, Heath & Co., 57
Wick China Co., 155
Wien, E., 42
Wiesbaden, 43
Wild, T. & Co., 61
Wildblood, Heath & Sons, 61
Wileman & Co., 61
Wilkinson & Delamain, 83
Wilkinson, A. J., 49
Willetts Mfg. Co., 155
Williams & Reppert, 155
Williamson, H. M. & Sons, 61

Willow Pattern, 50
Wilson, D. & Sons, 57
Wilson, R., 57, 58
Wiltshaw & Robinson, 70
Wingender, Chas., & Brother, 155
Winkle, F. & Co., 57
Winterthur, 101
Witteburg, 43
Wittenberger, 43
Wolfe & Hamilton, 71
Wolfe, Thomas, 71
Wolff, 108
Wolfsohn, 30, 31
Wood, 155
Wood & Barker, 49
Wood & Brownfield, 53
Wood & Caldwell, 49
Wood, Enoch & Sons, 49
Wood, J. B. & Co., 61
Wood, Ralph, 49
Wood & Son, 49
Woodruff, Madison, 155
Worcester, 50, 63, 76-79
Wores, H., 155
Works, Laban H., 155
Worthington, Humble & Holland, 60
Wrotham, 79
Würzburg, 43

Xrouet, 19

Yarmouth, 79
Young Bros., 82
Young, William, 63
Young, W. & Sons, 155
Yvermel, 19

Zaragoza, 111
Zell, 43
Ziegler, 25
Znaim, 43
Zoar Pottery, 155
Zsolnay, W., 32
Zurich, 114